THE CHESAPEAKE CAMPAIGN, 1813–14

CASEMATE | ILLUSTRATED

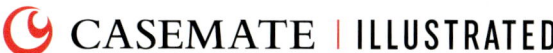

THE CHESAPEAKE CAMPAIGN, 1813–14

Charles P. Neimeyer

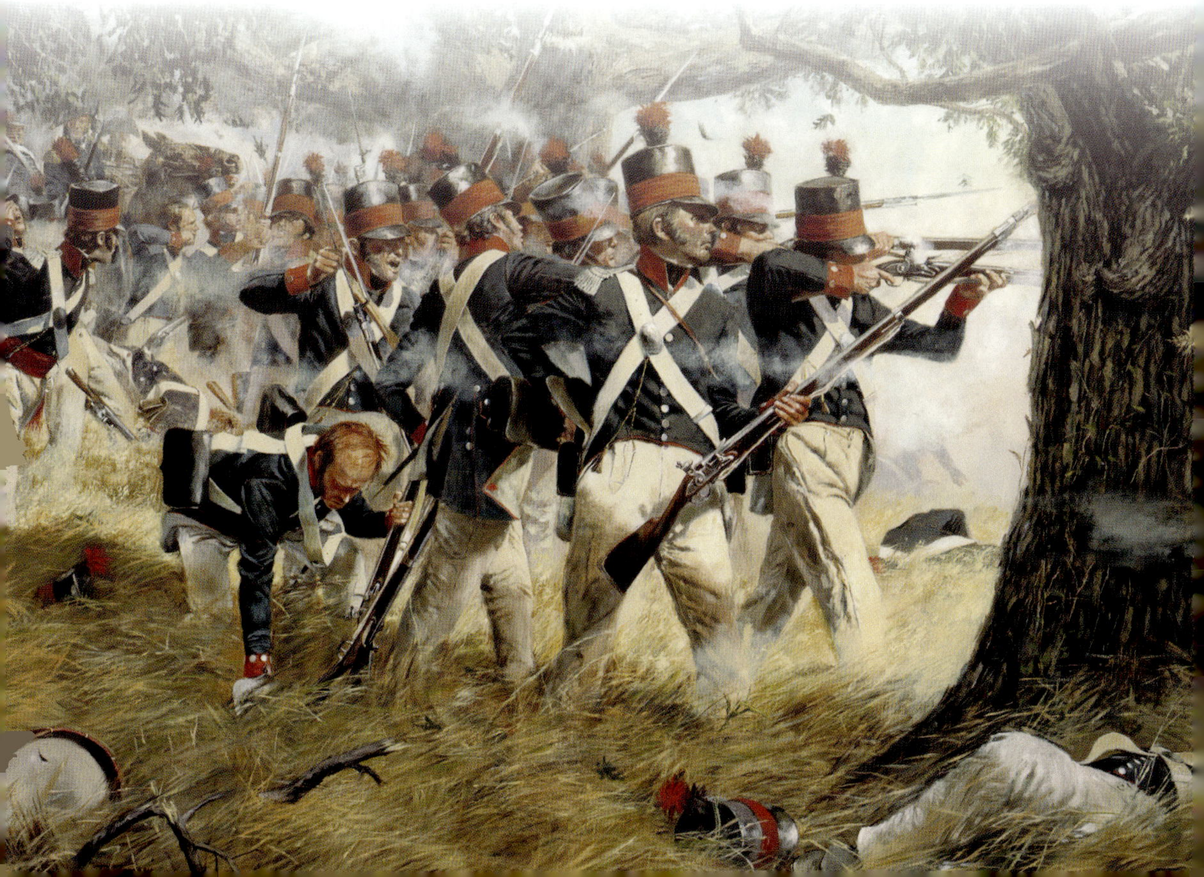

CIS0059

Published in 2025 by
CASEMATE PUBLISHERS
1950 Lawrence Road, Havertown, PA 19083, USA
and
47 Church Street, Barnsley, S70 2AS, UK

Main text, Center of Military History, United States Army, Washington, D.C., 2013
Boxed text, captions, and timeline by Chris McNab © Casemate Publishers 2025

Paperback edition: ISBN 978-1-63624-540-9
Digital edition: ISBN 978-1-63624-541-6

A CIP record for this book is available from the British Library.

All rights reserved. No part of this book may be reproduced or transmitted in any form or by any means, electronic or mechanical including photocopying, recording or by any information storage and retrieval system, without permission from the publisher in writing.

Maps by Myriam Bell
Design by Myriam Bell
Printed and bound in the United Kingdom by Short Run Press

For a complete list of Casemate titles, please contact:

CASEMATE PUBLISHERS (US)
Telephone (610) 853-9131
Fax (610) 853-9146
Email: casemate@casematepublishers.com
www.casematepublishers.com

CASEMATE PUBLISHERS (UK)
Telephone (0)1226 734350
Email: casemate@casemateuk.com
www.casemateuk.com

The Publisher's authorised representative in the EU for product safety is Authorised Rep Compliance Ltd., Ground Floor, 71 Lower Baggot Street, Dublin D02 P593, Ireland.
www.arccompliance.com

Contents

Timeline 6
The Fighting Begins 10
The Battles of Craney Island and
Hampton 19
Operations During the Remainder
of 1813 28
The 1814 Campaign Begins 37
The Battle of Bladensburg,
August 24, 1814 50
Plans and Preparations 62
The Battle of Baltimore,
September 12–14, 1814 73
Analysis 92
Further Reading 94
Index 95

Timeline

Fate had not been kind to the United States after it had declared war on Great Britain in June of 1812. During the ensuing six months, the British had not only repulsed several American attempts to invade Upper and Lower Canada, but had also captured some U.S. territory. By year's end, British Canada stood defiant, while America's military and political leadership wallowed in recrimination, frustration, and doubt. Britain's prospects in Canada, however, were by no means bright. The U.S. Army was growing in size and capability, deploying ever more soldiers to the Canadian frontier. In contrast, British North America was still thinly defended, as the vast majority of Britain's army remained in Europe fighting against the French Emperor Napoleon. As they examined the prospects for 1813, Britain's leaders searched for a way both to divert American regulars from the Canadian border and to put pressure on the United States to come to terms. A naval blockade offered one way to achieve these goals, but America's coastline was so long that it seemed best to concentrate on one area until the Royal Navy could free more ships from the war in Europe. The area the British government selected was the Chesapeake Bay.

1812

December — British Secretary of State for War and the Colonies, Lord Henry Bathurst, orders a limited blockade of the American coast, with particular attention to the Chesapeake Bay.

1813

February — Lead elements of the British blockading force arrived at the mouth of the bay, beginning a two-year campaign.

February 8 — British frigates captured the privateer *Lottery* attempting to run the blockade.

April — R. Adm. George Cockburn leads a series of raids on the towns of the upper Chesapeake.

June 22	The battle of Craney Island: American forces repel a British effort to attack the Gosport Navy Yard in Portsmouth and capture the frigate U.S.S. *Constellation*.
May	A deputation from Washington, Georgetown, and Alexandria urges the federal government to improve their defenses.
August 13	The British seize Queenstown.

1814

June	The British raid Benedict, Maryland, then penetrate upriver to Lower Marlboro, dispersing the local militia without a fight.
July 2	The British, after a brief skirmish with American troops, capture and lay waste town of St. Leonard.
August 6	Cockburn pushes up Virginia's Coan River, where the Lancaster County militia put up resistance before withdrawing.
August 19	Ross' army began an unopposed landing at Benedict, and all were ashore the following day.
August 22	The Chesapeake Bay Flotilla under Master Commandant Joshua Barney is scuttled following clashes with the Royal Navy.
August 24	The battle of Bladensburg results in a serious American defeat and opens the way for Maj. Gen. Robert Ross' British forces to enter Washington.
August 28	Fort Washington is destroyed by its own garrison and abandoned. Also on this day, the mayor and city leaders of Alexandria surrender the city.
September 12	The battle of North Point. American forces are defeated at North Point, Maryland, but they retreat in good order and Ross is killed in the battle.
September 12–15	The battle of Baltimore. In a pivotal moment in the War of 1812, American forces defeat a major British effort to capture Baltimore from land and sea.

The Chesapeake Campaign, 1813–14

The battle of Virginia Capes took place in September 1781 around the mouth of Chesapeake Bay. Although this engagement pre-dates the War of 1812, this artwork gives a powerful impression of naval engagements in the age of sail, the opponents presenting their thunderous broadsides to the enemy. (U.S. Navy Naval History and Heritage Command)

Timeline

The Fighting Begins

Situated between the states of Maryland and Virginia, the Chesapeake Bay was America's largest estuary. The bay and the watershed it served were home to vibrant agricultural and fishing activities; important ports (Baltimore, Maryland, and Norfolk, Virginia); a major naval construction yard at Portsmouth, Virginia; and last but not least, the nation's capital, Washington, D.C. Threaten these, the British reasoned, and America might shift its focus from trying to conquer Canada to defending its own homeland. Consequently, in December 1812 the British Secretary of State for War and the Colonies, Lord Henry Bathurst, directed Adm. Sir John Borlase Warren to impose a limited blockade of the American coast, with particular attention to the Chesapeake Bay. The lead elements of the British blockading force arrived at the mouth of the bay in February 1813 to begin what would become a two-year campaign.

▶ This plan of Portsmouth Harbor in Virginia, as seen towards the end of the Revolutionary War, gives a good impression of how fortifications were emplaced to straddle the waterway. (Library of Congress/PD)

▼ Henry Bathurst, 3rd Earl Bathurst, was the British Secretary of State for War and the Colonies between June 1812 and April 1827. (National Portrait Gallery/PD)

The initial action of the campaign occurred on February 8 when British frigates captured the privateer *Lottery* attempting to run the blockade. The ship became the first of many prizes the Royal Navy would seize during the following two summers. Warren's advance frigates effectively closed the *Chesapeake* to American shipping, and even the most daring privateers evaded his warships with difficulty. The blockade became even tighter in early March when R. Adm. George Cockburn joined Warren as his second in command, bringing with him additional ships.

The Fighting Begins

The Chesapeake Campaign, 1813–14

With even more ships sailing for North America, First Sea Lord Robert Dundas, the 2d Viscount Melville, counseled Warren not to concentrate overly on the Chesapeake Bay; but Portsmouth's strategically important Gosport Navy Yard, located near Norfolk, proved too tempting a target to ignore. At anchor within the harbor was one of America's major warships, the frigate U.S.S. *Constellation*, guarded by over three thousand Virginia militiamen, numerous gunboats, and two major fortifications, Forts Norfolk and Nelson. With few marines to act as land troops, Warren needed British Army assistance. While waiting for troops to arrive, the energetic Cockburn used ship's boats and barges to enter bay tributaries, where they captured many shallow-draft vessels to use in future operations.

By mid-April, one division of Warren's fleet took station off the Elizabeth River to blockade *Constellation*, while Cockburn led the other on a series of raids on the towns of the upper Chesapeake (see Map 1). On the sixteenth, his squadron demonstrated off the mouth of the Patapsco River, the gateway to Baltimore. Cockburn meant the

▲ John Borlase Warren, by Daniel Orme. (Österreichische Nationalbibliothek/PD)

▼ This artwork, displayed in Naval Air Station Patuxent River, depicts a British raid on coastal villages around Chesapeake Bay in 1813. (U.S. Navy)

The Fighting Begins

display to hold the attention of the militia commander in the region, Maj. Gen. Samuel Smith, before sailing farther north. For the rest of the month, Cockburn sent expeditions of sailors and marines ashore, supported by warships and auxiliary vessels, to raid small port towns. He established a policy that "should resistance be made, I shall consider [what I take] as a prize of war." If a town submitted, however, he left its homes and other structures mostly intact. Although he claimed to have paid for any confiscated property, he usually did so with notes that could only be redeemed after the war.

Cockburn struck first on the Elk River at the extreme northeastern corner of the bay. After overcoming some ineffective militia at Frenchtown, Maryland, on April 29, he burned the depot there before turning toward Elkton, Maryland. There, however, the militia-manned battery—later named Fort Defiance—successfully repelled the British attack. Undeterred, Cockburn sailed toward Maryland's Western Shore in early May and anchored off Havre de Grace at the mouth of the Susquehanna River. An artillery battery defended the seaward approach to the prosperous village of about sixty dwellings. Located on the southern outskirts, the fortification, called the Potato Battery, stood on Concord Point. The battery opened fire as the landing barges and a boat armed with Congreve rockets approached in the early morning of May 3, but British return fire forced most of the militia to abandon the position.

▼ George Cockburn, engraving by Charles Turner. (Library of Congress)

Developed by William Congreve of the Royal Arsenal, British Congreve rockets comprised a three-foot iron tube containing black powder propellant topped by a conical or spherical shell that contained explosive, musket balls, or incendiary materiel. The entire apparatus was affixed to a fifteen-foot-long stabilizing pole. The noisy missiles proved most effective in unnerving unseasoned troops and setting buildings on fire. Although they rarely caused casualties, one struck and killed a Havre de Grace militiaman.

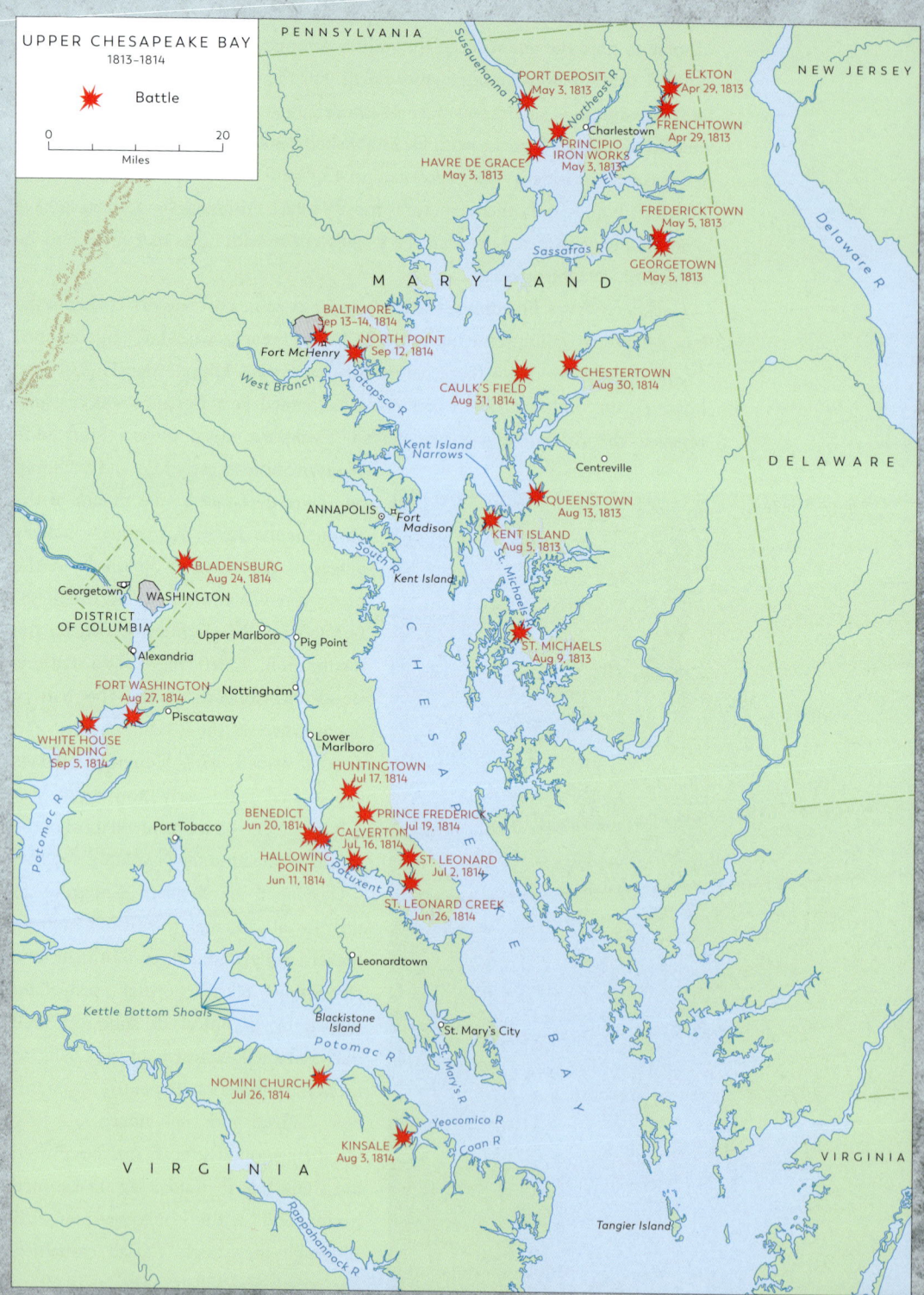

▲ Map 1

The Fighting Begins

Despite Cockburn's threats of punishing resistance, Lt. John O'Neill remained at his Potato Battery post and defiantly fired its cannon until he was injured. O'Neill and two other men were captured and briefly taken prisoner. Since the militia had opposed the landing and the town refused Cockburn's ransom demand of $20,000, a British officer informed town leaders that "your village shall now feel the effects of war." British sailors and marines looted and burned most of the town's structures, including the home of Commodore John Rodgers, U.S. Navy, but neighbors extinguished the blaze before it did much damage.

Cockburn next sent an expedition up the Susquehanna River to burn a warehouse at Smith's, or Bell's, Ferry, but was deterred from landing at Port Deposit across the Susquehanna by a battery manned by militia. Cockburn then targeted the nearby Principio Iron Works on the Northeast River. Described as "one of the most valuable Works of [its] kind in America," with one of the few cannon foundries in the country, it represented the most significant target in the region. The raiders destroyed at least forty-six cannon, including twenty-eight 32-pounders ready for shipment.

▼ A memorial to Lt. John O'Neill, topped by a cannon from the War of 1812, marks the site of the Concord Point battery in Havre de Grace. (Diiscool/PD)

Profile:
Sir William Congreve (1772–1828)

Sir William Congreve lived a life of politics, commerce, and invention, although he is primarily and justifiably remembered for the latter. He was born on May 17, 1772 into a noble and military family, his father being Lt. Gen. Sir William Congreve, 1st Baronet. Notably, given his son's later direction, Congreve senior served as both deputy comptroller and later the comptroller of the Woolwich Royal Laboratory, during which time he made advances in the production and quality of gunpowder. William Congreve junior had evident intellect, graduating from Trinity College, Cambridge, with both BA and MA degrees in Law. In the early years of the 19th century, he dipped his toe into military service as a volunteer for the London and Westminster Light Horse, but also pursued a failed and ultimately libelous career in polemical publishing. He subsequently directed his focus on inventing, with a leaning (although far from exclusively) towards military weapons. His most famous invention is certainly the Congreve rocket, but he also designed a time fuze and a gun recoil system. Like his father, he became comptroller of the Royal Laboratory at Woolwich; he took the position in 1814, the year his father died, and held it until his own death. Congreve's career appeared destined for steady success, receiving a variety of orders and honors. But his subsequent and shady international business dealings led to a prosecution for fraud in 1826, which he handled badly by fleeing to France, where he died on May 16, 1828.

▲ This 1804 artwork of William Congreve shows one of his legendary Congreve rockets burning its way into the sky from an elevated wooden launcher, the inventor apparently shielding his eyes from the glare. (Richie Bendall)

Cockburn then weighed anchor and returned to the Eastern Shore of the Chesapeake Bay. The citizens of Georgetown and Fredericktown, twin communities on opposite banks of the Sassafras River, feared the worst as British ships approached on May 5. Cockburn dispatched a raiding force accompanied by three small support vessels and a rocket boat, and sent two captured slaves ashore under a white flag to deliver his offer to spare the towns if they surrendered. Col. Thomas W. Veazey of the 49th Maryland Regiment, however, manned a breastwork at the narrowest part of the river at Pearce Point armed with a 6-pounder cannon and only a few rounds of ammunition. The British opened fire with cannon and Congreve rockets and landed marines to outflank the American battery. The invaders suffered five wounded, but forced the militia to retreat, which left both towns defenseless. Due to the resistance, Cockburn ordered his men to loot the area and put both towns to the torch. The master's log

The naval blockade

Naval blockade was a centerpiece strategy of the British government during the War of 1812, one with significant impact on the progression of the conflict. Five years prior to the outbreak of the war, in 1807, Britain was locked into its long-running war with Napoleonic France. Part of British strategic policy was to use its powerful navy to stop, inspect and, if necessary, seize merchant shipping bound for French territories or exporting to continental France. When war with America broke out in 1812, therefore, the instruments and tactics of blockade were already understood. The British government declared an official blockade in November 1812, and by February 1813 it extended from the Delaware to the Chesapeake Bays. The intention was simple: strangle the American economy and foster internal dissent amongst the enemy.

The blockade was tightened and widened implacably as the war progressed, in terms of both the number of Royal Navy vessels deployed and the extent of the coastline covered. In 1811, just before war began, there were a total of 20 British ships on station off North America, but by 1814 there were 135 vessels, monitoring the entire U.S. coastline south of Rhode Island. The economic impact of the blockade was profound. It reduced the total value of imports and exports into North America from a pre-war figure of $114 million to just $20 million, with miserable effects on American standards of living and the livelihoods of coastal communities.

The Chesapeake Campaign, 1813–14

◀ On April 3, 1813, the boats of the British squadron in Chesapeake Bay pursued four large American schooners 15 miles up Rappahannock River. The American privateer schooner *Dolphin*, with 12 guns and 98 men, was boarded and captured. (Mariners' Museum, Bailey Collection, #423)

of H.M.S. *Maidstone* recorded that "the fires from what had once been the ports of Fredericktown and Georgetown could be seen from the decks" ten miles away. In response, American newspapers called Cockburn's men a "tiger banditti," and Charlestown, on the Northeast River, sent a deputation to assure the admiral that he would encounter no resistance, which was exactly the effect that Cockburn had hoped. Its mission largely accomplished, the squadron returned to the mouth of Chesapeake Bay, where Admiral Warren was massing for the long-awaited assault on Norfolk.

◀ *British Burning of Havre de Grace*, by William Charles. (Maryland Historical Society)

The Battles of Craney Island and Hampton

What made the attack on Norfolk possible was the arrival from Bermuda in May of the British Army's 102d Regiment of Foot, a company of Royal Artillery, two Independent Companies of Foreigners, and two battalions of Royal Marines. Col. Sir Thomas S. Beckwith, a veteran of Britain's war against Napoleon, commanded the troops. The independent companies were composed of highly fractious men who proved to be troublesome.

Led by British officers, their ranks included men of various nationalities, mostly French, who had been captured on European battlefields and who had elected to serve in the British Army rather than remain prisoners of war. Lt. Col. Charles Napier's 102d Regiment of Foot also possessed a less-than-stellar pedigree. Originally formed in 1789 as the New South Wales Corps to garrison Australia, it had once served as a penal regiment for soldiers court-martialed in other units. After recruiting "150 lads born in the Colony [Australia] of free birth and good character," the unit had returned to England in 1810, where it had been reconstituted as the 102d Regiment of Foot. By the summer, Warren had over twenty-four hundred soldiers and marines under his command, which he believed sufficient to seize Norfolk.

The town's defenses—at Craney Island at the mouth of the Elizabeth River and at two forts located closer to the city—were considerable. The federal government had neglected the two Revolutionary War–era forts until 1794, when Congress had appropriated $3,000 to repair Fort Nelson on the west bank of the Elizabeth River at Windmill Point and to rebuild Fort Norfolk on the east. In 1813, Fort Nelson had parapets "14 feet high and walls that were 15 feet thick with embrasures for 42 guns" facing the water, but was considerably weaker on its landward side (Map 2).

The Chesapeake Campaign, 1813–14

Due to the importance of Gosport Navy Yard, twenty-one gunboats augmented the region's defenses. President Thomas Jefferson's controversial policy was the building of low-cost gunboats for coastal defense instead of deep-water warships. Each gunboat measured between fifty to seventy-five feet long and was propelled by sails and oars. The boats mounted either one 24- or 32-pounder gun in the bow on a carriage and two 12-pounder carronades, one on each side.

The American militia's commanding officer, Brig. Gen. Robert B. Taylor, complained that "the Gun Boats are most wretchedly manned ... and should they fall into the Enemy's hands ... they will be turned against us." *Constellation*'s commander, Capt. Charles Stewart, echoed Taylor's complaints to Secretary of the Navy William Jones, adding that "to protect their falling into their hands, I was under the necessity of withdrawing them within the fortifications of Norfolk." Of twenty-one gunboats, Stewart and Navy Yard Superintendent Capt. John Cassin could only man seven.

By early June, the Secretary of the Navy ordered Stewart to take command of the frigate *Constitution*, and temporarily replaced him with Master Commandant Joseph Tarbell. Captain Cassin, now the senior naval officer in the area,

▲ William Jones had been a successful politician and businessman by the time he was appointed as the U.S. Secretary of the Navy on May 9, 1813, an office he held until February 8, 1814. (U.S. Naval History and Heritage Command)

◀ The frigate U.S.S. *Constitution*, here shown escaping a British squadron in 1812, was launched in 1797 and has served the United States for more than 200 years—the surviving vessel was designated America's Ship of State in 2009 and today more than 500,000 people a year visit the vessel in Boston. (Library of Congress/PD)

The Battles of Craney Island and Hampton

repositioned the gunboats toward the mouth of the Elizabeth River and forward of the line of sunken hulks blocking the channel. They formed a mutually supporting defensive arc that extended from Lambert's Point on the east bank to low-lying Craney Island on the west. Meanwhile, the War Department had assigned Capt. Walter K. Armistead of the U.S. Army Corps of Engineers to begin construction of fortifications on the southeast part of Craney Island facing the channel and to dig trenches at its vulnerable northwest corner. General Taylor assigned Lt. Col. Henry Beatty to command the post and its garrison of about four hundred fifty men. Maj. James Faulkner commanded all the artillery on Craney Island. He had

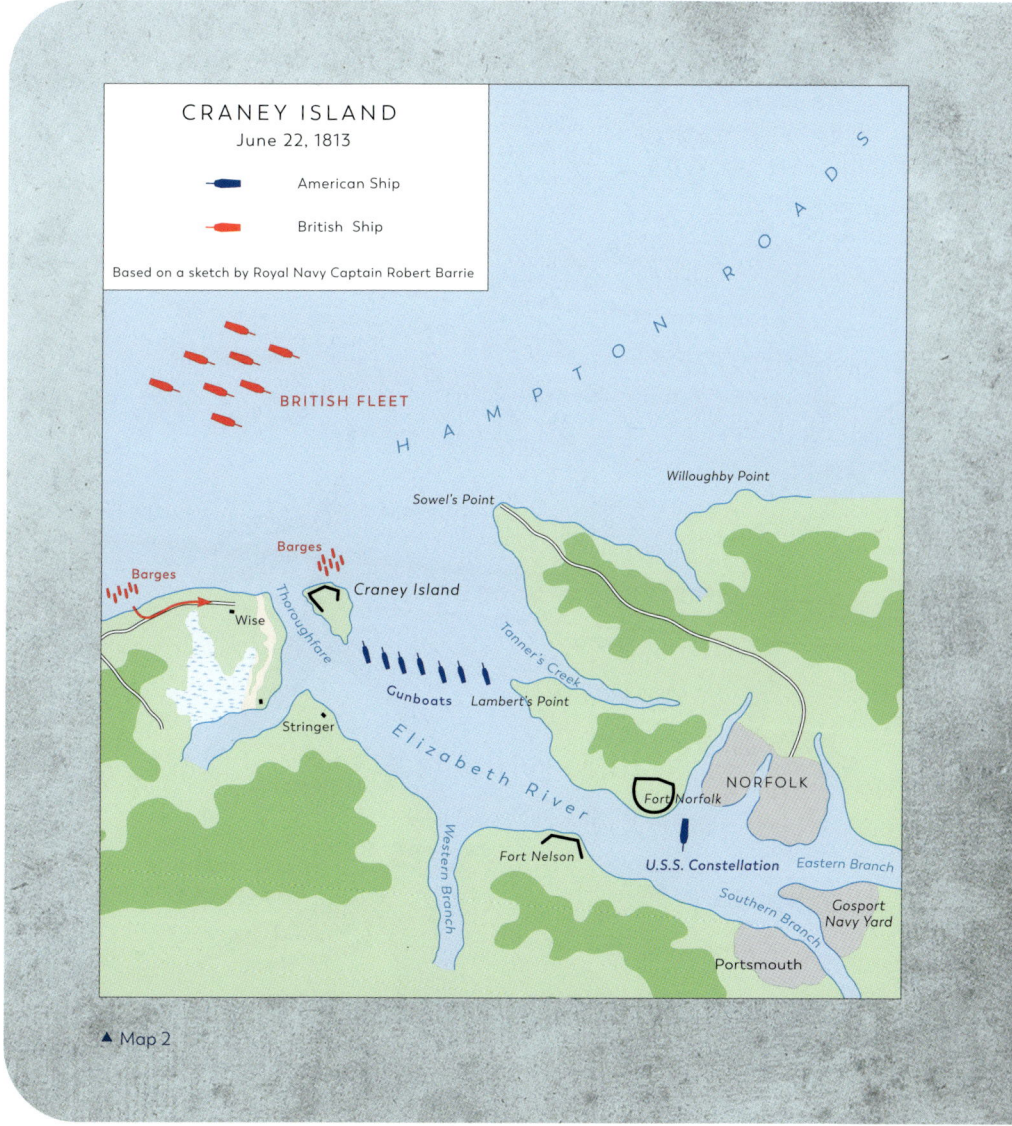

▲ Map 2

The Chesapeake Campaign, 1813–14

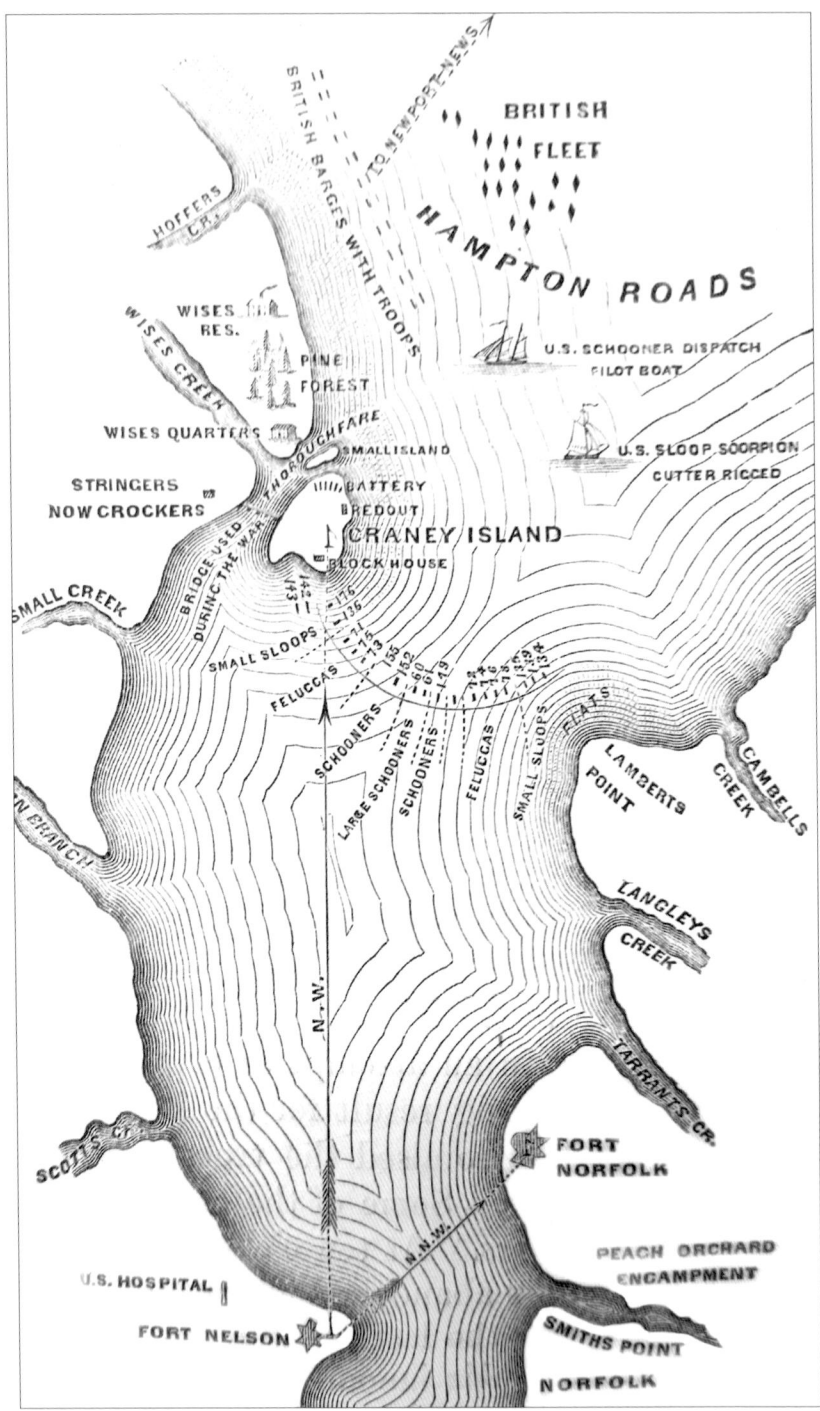

▲ A detailed pictorial map of the battle of Craney Island, fought on June 22, 1813. The American defenders managed to repel the British amphibious assault this time, although the British returned to campaign into the Chesapeake Bay the following year. (Benson Lossing/PD)

two heavy naval 24-pounders and one 18-pounder positioned in the unfinished fort, augmented with Capt. Arthur Emmerson's Portsmouth Light Artillery company with four 6-pounder field guns and Capt. John Richardson's Charlotte County Light Artillery acting as infantry. Maj. Andrew Waggoner commanded the infantry, which included his own battalion of the 4th Virginia Regiment and Capt. Thomas Robert's company of riflemen.

When they saw British masts approximately five miles away on June 20, 1813, the Americans knew that the long-expected attack was imminent. The next day, Taylor reinforced the defenders with Capt. Richard Pollard's company of regulars from the 20th U.S. Infantry, Capt. Jesse Naille's detachment of the 5th Virginia Regiment, and a detachment of riflemen from the 3d Virginia Regiment commanded by Ens. Archibald Atkinson. Tarbell sent about one hundred sailors commanded by Lt. B. J. Neale to provide crews for the great guns and fifty marines under Lt. Henry Breckinridge to reinforce the infantry. Beatty then had about seven hundred forty men to oppose Warren's soldiers and marines. Orderly Sgt. James Jarvis noted that all "arrangements thus made to defend the post, we waited the approach of the enemy and felt we were prepared to give them a decent reception for our troops were full of ardor."

During the early morning hours of June 22, the alarm gun sounded after an alert, albeit jittery, sentry on Craney Island thought he saw a boat moving near the Thoroughfare, a narrow strait between the island and mainland. Although the illusion proved to be floating debris, the entire garrison was ready for action as dawn broke. By that time, the Americans clearly saw redcoats landing and assembling across the water at the nearby Wise farm. Colonel Beatty arranged his infantry into a line that faced the Thoroughfare on the northwestern part of the island. Major Faulkner's artillerymen—without oxen or horses—manhandled the heavy naval guns to the threatened part of the island and combined them into a single battery with Emmerson's 6-pounders.

Beckwith's regiment provided the bulk of the British landing force. He had planned the landing at Wise farm as a diversion, while another detachment crossed Wise Harr to the Stringer farm on the western side of Craney Island. Meanwhile, additional barges carried soldiers and marines for a direct assault against the island's northwestern beaches. The plan went wrong when the British discovered that neither Wise Creek nor the Thoroughfare was fordable. Beckwith's troops, unable to cross, massed on the riverbank. In order to draw the American artillerymen's attention away from this lucrative target, Beckwith had the supporting Congreve rocket batteries, located near a building on the Wise farm, fire their noisy missiles. They drew accurate American counterbattery fire that destroyed the building and caused a number of casualties. British soldiers who fled from the cover of the building were subjected to canister and grapeshot from Faulkner's guns.

The Chesapeake Campaign, 1813–14

As this carnage took place, the main British assault force of fifteen hundred soldiers and marines approached the northwestern shore of Craney Island in fifty barges. Led by Admiral Warren's personal barge, named *Centipede* for its bright-green color and numerous oars, the British landing craft began to close on the island at 1100. Warren's flag captain, Capt. Samuel G. Pechell of H.M.S. *San Domingo*, commanded the amphibious force. He had attempted to time his assault with Beckwith's flank attack, unaware that it had already been smashed by Faulkner's artillery. As Pechell's men moved toward the beach, Faulkner's gun crews focused attention on this new threat. They held their fire until the barges were well within range, at which point the artillerymen fired a deadly volley. Most of the barges grounded on unseen mudflats about three hundred yards from shore as the Americans poured shot after shot into them. Men who jumped over the sides of their barges sunk knee-deep into the muck. Standing in *Centipede*, Royal Navy Capt. J. M. Hanchett tried to rally his men when a shot smashed through the hull and severely wounded him in the thigh. Hanchett and his men abandoned *Centipede*, while nearby barges recovered survivors as best they could. Pechell ordered a retreat back to the ships, and Warren directed the troops in the vicinity of Wise farm to return to their ships as well. The Americans had won.

Faulkner allowed a group of sailors to take the grounded *Centipede* as a prize. Although hulled in a few places, the damaged barge was quickly repaired. As the British withdrew, many defenders waded into the mudflats to take potshots at the fleeing enemy, giving rise to a British claim that the Americans had gone into the flats to kill the wounded left behind. Evidence that such occurred is lacking, while Midshipman Josiah Tatnall of *Constellation* wrote that his men brought a number of British wounded ashore in hammocks for medical treatment.

◀ This fine artwork from 1814 illustrates the tactical applications of Congreve rockets in a naval context. As well as delivering ship-to-ship fire, the Congreve rockets were also used to deliver offshore bombardments of coastal positions. (National Maritime Museum, Greenwich/PD)

The Battles of Craney Island and Hampton

▲ Captain George Richard Pechell entered the Royal Navy in 1803 and made captain by 1826 and vice admiral by 1858. He also served as a Whig Member of Parliament (MP) for the constituency of Brighton, UK, for 25 years. (National Maritime Museum, Greenwich/PD)

A thrilled Captain Cassin wrote to Secretary of the Navy Jones that the gun crew from *Constellation* "fired their [cannon] more like riflemen than Artillerists," but he did not mention the role Virginia militia had played at all. In contrast, Colonel Beatty praised all the participating units in his report, including the few gunboats that had briefly engaged British barges. The Americans reported no casualties, while the British suffered at least sixteen men killed and sixty-two missing.

Stymied at Norfolk, Admiral Warren turned his attention across Hampton Roads to Hampton, Virginia, because he believed the town "commanded communication between [the] upper country and Norfolk" (Map 3). Unlike at Craney Island, the British did not have to contend with river forts, gunboats, or sunken hulks. The numerous undefended inlets just west of town made Hampton especially vulnerable to an amphibious attack. Cockburn positioned his ships off Blackbeard's Point near Newport News. A joint force consisting of marines under Lt. Col. Richard Williams and soldiers of Beckwith's regiment, nearly two thousand men, landed about two miles west of Hampton near the home of Daniel Murphy on June 25. As the landing party advanced eastward on the Celey Road, Cockburn's small craft fired their cannon at a militia camp and artillery battery commanded by Capt. Brazure W. Pryor, located at a farm called Little England, just southwest of and separated from Hampton by a small creek. Maj. Stapleton Crutchfield, commanding about four hundred fifty militiamen, later reported that Pryor's guns repelled the British "in a manner worthy of veteran troops." Cockburn's actions, however, were merely a diversion to allow Williams' and Beckwith's troops to arrive on Crutchfield's right flank.

A militia rifle company, commanded by Capt. Richard B. Servant, guarding the Celey Road observed and reported that the British troops were advancing from the west. Crutchfield immediately sent reinforcements, only to be ambushed as they approached the wood line that flanked the road. Sergeant Jarvis described, "We advanced in column of platoons, thro' a lane and open cornfield which led from our encampment ... to the main and Ceyle [sic] Roads. When in the field within 200 yards of the gate opening into the Ceyley [sic] road and a thicket of pine, we were fired upon by the enemy's musketry from a thick wood at the upper end of a field." Jarvis continued, "orders were given to wheel to the left into line and march

25

upon the enemy." Advancing less than fifty yards, "the enemy opened upon us two six-pound field pieces loaded with grape and canister shot and his machines filled with rockets of a small size."

Confused fighting raged in the woods that separated the Celey Road and the main militia camp until the British landed some light field guns and fired grapeshot into Crutchfield's men, sending the Americans in full flight through Hampton and northward on the road toward Yorktown, Virginia. Just before being overrun, Pryor's artillerymen spiked their guns and swam the creek to avoid capture. The British reported only five men killed, thirty-three wounded, and ten missing. The militia lost seven dead, twelve wounded, and eleven missing.

As most of the inhabitants fled Hampton, British soldiers looted private homes and harassed civilians. The British claimed the depredations were committed in revenge for the Americans allegedly firing on their wounded at Craney Island. Officers confirmed that their men committed a number of crimes, but were nearly unanimous in blaming the green-coated Independent Companies of Foreigners for the most egregious conduct. Colonel Beckwith noted that with "their dispersing to plunder in every direction, [and] their Brutal treatment of several peaceable Inhabitants," their officers "found it impossible to Check Them." The independent companies' behavior failed to improve, as he stated, "Since their return on board, their conduct has been uniformly the Same and ... have not hesitated to say, that when next landed, they would choose a Service for themselves [desert]." The colonel sent them to Halifax, Nova Scotia.

▼ A substantial blockhouse construction on Craney Island; note the apertures for delivering outgoing cannon and musket fire around the upper floor. (Benson John Lossing, *Harper's Encyclopedia of United States History*, Vol 2, 1912. Courtesy FCIT, https://etc.usf.edu/clipart)

▲ Map 3

Operations During the Remainder of 1813

Not yet prepared to quit the operations for the season, V. Adm. Sir Alexander Cochrane sent Cockburn in H.M.S. *Scepter* with a detachment of ships and elements of Beckwith's regiment to raid Ocracoke and Portsmouth Islands, North Carolina. The foray netted two privateers.

While Cockburn was away, Warren ordered Capt. William H. Shirreff of H.M.S. *Barrossa* to take his frigate, four shallow-draft vessels, and a landing force of six hundred men up the Potomac River toward Washington, D.C. Except as the seat of government, the city had little military value and, therefore, its defenses were

▼ A modern-day view of the waters around Portsmouth, North Carolina, specifically Coast Guard Creek looking northeast from the lookout tower of the U.S. Life-Saving Station. Pamlico Sound is the main body of water beyond, the entrance to which is Ocracoke Inlet, bounded by Portsmouth Island and Ocracoke Island. (Jarek Tuszyński)

Profile:
Vice Admiral Alexander Cochrane (1758–1832)

▼ Vice Admiral Alexander Cochrane. The criticisms he attracted after the British defeat at New Orleans were not helped by the fact that one of the casualties was the Duke of Wellington's brother-in-law. (National Galleries of Scotland/PD)

Alexander Inglis Cochrane was born on April 23, 1758, the son of the Scottish 8th Earl of Dundonald. As the sixth son of eight, titular inheritance was unlikely, so instead Cochrane joined the Royal Navy as a boy, looking to forge greatness via feats of arms rather than by dint of ancestry. It was a fortuitous choice. By 1778 he was a lieutenant and had been blooded in the naval engagements of the American Revolution. He soon took the first of a series of captaincies, earning particular distinction as a hunter of French privateers. The French Revolutionary and Napoleonic wars gave Cochrane further leadership and combat opportunities in Egypt, the West Indies and the Caribbean. He stood out as one of Britain's most competent naval tacticians; in 1804 he was promoted to rear admiral, and vice admiral in 1810.

In 1814, Cochrane was appointed Commander in Chief of the North America Station, tasked with the ruthless naval blockade of the United States during the War of 1812. He pursed this campaign with unforgiving drive, especially around the Chesapeake Bay. The later British defeat in the battle of New Orleans in January 1815—a campaign mismanaged by Cochrane—took some of the shine off his reputation. Nevertheless, back in England after the war, he was promoted Admiral of the Blue in 1819 and served as Commander in Chief at Plymouth from 1821 until his retirement 1824. Cochrane died on January 26, 1832, ironically in Paris, the capital of the country he spent much of his service career seeking to defeat.

The Chesapeake Campaign, 1813–14

less robust than those at Norfolk or Baltimore. Many believed that the capital's protection rested in its largely inaccessible geographic location. An invading fleet had to travel against a strong current and avoid treacherous shoals just to come within sight of the city. Warren hoped threatening the national capital might compel the Americans to detach forces from the Canadian border. While the approaching British did cause the mobilization of local militia, the U.S. government did not redeploy any Regular Army units from the Canadian border. Secretary of War John Armstrong did, however, direct the 36th and 38th U.S. Infantry to Fort Washington, Maryland, overlooking the Potomac at Digges Point a few miles south of the capital district.

Originally named Fort Warburton, Fort Washington was the only fortification guarding the river approaches to Washington, D.C. Capt. George Bomford, its chief engineer, conceded that the post had significant deficiencies. Based on the plan used for Fort Madison at Annapolis, Maryland, the dimensions proved too large for the four acres at Digges Point. He lamented that "Fort Washington was really an attempt to adopt a standard plan to an unsuitable site. It therefore violated a fundamental rule—the fort must suit its site." Having no alternative, Bomford altered the plan, reducing the number of guns to fifteen, half as many it needed to be effective. Furthermore, the site did not allow enough room for barracks to house more than the regular artillerymen to man the guns facing the water, and relied on militia to defend the landward side.

Aware that the fort would not stop a waterborne attack, in May 1813 a deputation of citizens from the three major towns in the District of Columbia—Washington, Georgetown, and Alexandria—had urged the federal government to improve the defenses. Secretary of War Armstrong had sent Col. Decius Wadsworth, the Army's Commissary General of Ordnance, to investigate. He had concluded that neither a further reinforcement of heavy guns nor the construction of auxiliary batteries was necessary, as the challenges posed by navigating the Potomac provided enough protection. Maj. Gen. James Wilkinson had disagreed, remarking that Fort Washington "could easily be knocked out either by the guns of a frigate or taken by a landing force at night from the back." Lt. Edmund Kennedy, commanding the Potomac Flotilla of gunboats, had likewise written Secretary of the Navy Jones on April 13 that "one Gun Boat well mann'd might attack it in the present Situation with certain Success."

As it turned out, Wilkinson's and Kennedy's concerns and Armstrong's preparations proved unnecessary. On encountering the treacherous Kettle Bottom Shoals, forty miles from the city, the British had decided to return to the mouth of the Potomac. The stillborn probe notwithstanding, Cockburn landed about four hundred troops on Blackistone (St. Clement's) Island off the western shore of Chesapeake Bay near St. Mary's City, Maryland. He put the men to work digging

▶ This artwork shows typical American infantry uniform between 1813 and 1821. Regulations issued in February 1812 stated that there should be a single-breasted "coatee" with red collar and cuffs, but the red collar and cuffs were removed in revisions in May 1813. (Library of Congress/PD)

Operations During the Remainder of 1813

Profile:
James Monroe (1758–1831)

Born on April 28, 1758, into a wealthy plantation family from Westmoreland, Virginia, James Monroe was in the midst of receiving an excellent education when the outbreak of war in 1775 set a new course for his life. He joined the 3d Virginia Infantry as a freshly commissioned lieutenant. As a combat officer, he fought in many major engagements of the War of Independence, including the battles of Brandywine, Monmouth and Trenton (he was wounded at the latter), and ended the war with the rank of lieutenant colonel. He also forged advantageous political and military connections, including with George Washington and Alexander Hamilton.

After the war, he initially returned to his studies in law, gaining the patronage of Virginia Governor Thomas Jefferson. His political career began in 1782, with his election to the Virginia House of Delegates. He subsequently held office as Senator for Virginia (1790–1794), U.S. Minister to France (1794–1796) and Britain (1803–1807), and, from April 1811, U.S. Secretary of State. He held this office until 1817, and during the War of 1812 he also became Secretary of War.

The apogee of his career was, of course, his eight years as U.S. President (1817–1825). His most famous historical legacy is the "Monroe Doctrine" of 1823, which barred the European powers from involving themselves in the affairs of the Western Hemisphere. Monroe died, with auspicious timing, on July 4, 1831, in New York City.

▲ James Monroe, by John Vanderlyn. (National Portrait Gallery, Smithsonian Institution/CC0)

wells for a convenient source of fresh water. When he heard of yet another British incursion into southern Maryland, Secretary of State James Monroe rode to personally reconnoiter, and requested Armstrong to send at least three hundred fifty regulars to drive off the enemy. Instead, the Secretary of War sent a small detachment, which failed to intimidate the British as they plundered St. Mary's, Charles, and Calvert Counties southeast of Washington.

On August 8, the British anchored fifteen ships off the mouth of the Patapsco River, appearing to threaten Baltimore again, but it proved to be a ruse. The British weighed anchor after a few days and headed south to threaten Annapolis. Considering the state capital too strongly defended, Cockburn established a base on the eastern side of the Chesapeake Bay at Kent Island, which permitted him to simultaneously threaten Baltimore and Annapolis. After driving off the local militia, the 102d Foot and a battalion of Royal Marines built huts for an extended stay.

Hearing rumors that there were two privateers under construction at the prosperous Eastern Shore town of St. Michaels, Maryland, the British planned a raid. On the evening of August 9, they embarked about three hundred troops in cutters and barges for a predawn attack that would catch the volunteer and drafted companies detached from the 12th Militia Brigade, under the command of Brig. Gen. Perry Benson, by surprise. Capt. Samuel Thomas of the Talbot Volunteer Artillery Company distributed his guns to several batteries. A four-gun battery commanded by Lt. William Dodson located at Parrott's Point constituted the town's principal defense, while Lt. John Graham commanded an auxiliary battery of two guns at the wharves. First Lt. Clement Vickers commanded two guns at Mill Point.

As the British approached to within thirty yards, Dodson's guns fired a single volley, which caused few casualties. British troops quickly overran the battery as the militiamen fled toward town. Vickers' two guns then opened fire on the British who, after observing no vessels in the harbor, destroyed the Parrott's Point battery and returned to their barges. By 1300, they headed back to Kent Island. The Americans suffered no losses, but claimed to have inflicted twenty-nine British casualties, although Cdr. Henry L. Baker of the Royal Navy reported only two wounded. While not substantiated, local tradition holds that inhabitants hung lanterns on the trees in the nearby woods to deceive the British about the actual location of the town.

A few days later, Cockburn went after a bigger target. The 38th Maryland Regiment had assembled near Queenstown, just a few miles across the Kent Island Narrows. The understrength Queen Anne County militia, commanded by Maj. William H. Nicholson, had an infantry battalion of 244 men; a cavalry unit of about 100 men under the command of Maj. Thomas Emory; and a 35-man artillery company with two 6-pounders commanded by Capt. Gustavus Wright. In

The Chesapeake Campaign, 1813–14

Operations During the Remainder of 1813

the early morning of August 13, a cavalry scout informed Nicholson that British troops had crossed the Kent Narrows and were headed toward Queenstown. Alerted, Nicholson prepared to resist the British advance. Concerned that the British would capture or destroy two companies of infantry, under the command of Capt. James Massey, positioned on the neck of land that separated his camp from the Kent Narrows, Nicholson feared the worst when he heard the sound of heavy musketry. During the ensuing skirmish at a defile near Slippery Hill, American fire killed two British soldiers and Beckwith's horse.

At about 0400, a scout reported that a number of barges had entered Queen Anne's Creek and three hundred British marines had landed at the Bowlingly Plantation. In fact, the British had mistakenly landed at Blakeford—the home of former Maryland governor Robert Wright—on the opposite shore. The error bought the militia time to escape being surrounded, and Nicholson ordered a retreat toward Centreville, which allowed the British to seize Queenstown

◀ In naval engagements, capture rather than destruction of the enemy vessels was often the preferred outcome. This artwork depicts the prelude to the gunnery battle between the frigates U.S.S. *Chesapeake* and H.M.S. *Shannon* on June 1, 1813 off Boston, in which the American ship was captured. (Library of Congress/PD)

without further resistance. The British did not burn Bowlingly, but looted several homes before withdrawing. With hurricane season approaching, and after another brief attempt at St. Michaels on August 26, Admiral Warren brought the campaign to a close. He established a small base on Tangier Island for the naval forces that would stay behind to maintain the blockade and to train the liberated and runaway slaves who agreed to join the Colonial Marines. In September, he sailed with the majority of his fleet to Halifax, while Cockburn took most of the rest to Bermuda for the winter. Although his squadron had spread terror throughout the region, Warren had failed to divert U.S. forces from Canada.

The 1814 Campaign Begins

Following Napoleon's defeat and exile to the island of Elba in early 1814, Great Britain could focus all of its military might against the United States. The Admiralty replaced Warren with the more aggressive Cochrane. The move pleased Cockburn, who possessed remarkable intelligence on the region and remained second in command. He believed that his new commander understood the need not only to defeat but also to punish the Americans. The performance of the supporting British troops the previous year had been disappointing, and Cockburn hoped the Crown would assign a more aggressive army commander as well.

American defenses on the Chesapeake remained weak. The United States continued to commit most of its newly raised Regular Army regiments to the Canadian theater, while the U.S.S. *Constellation* at Norfolk and the new sloops-of-war *Erie* and *Ontario* nearing completion at Baltimore remained blockaded. Only an ad hoc fleet of barges and sloops commanded by acting Master Commandant Joshua Barney operated on the waters of the bay. By late April 1814, its fifteen vessels, including the sloop-rigged gunboat *Scorpion* as flagship, moved to harass the British base on Tangier Island. Simultaneously, Col. Henry Carberry sent a detachment of his 36th U.S. Infantry to oppose British raids in the St. Leonard, Maryland, area. On seeing the regulars, many citizens assumed the government would finally take a stand.

Barney's flotilla attacked a number of smaller British vessels and forced them to flee southward to the safety of their warships. He pursued them until a ship-of-the-line bore down on his flotilla, which caused him to withdraw into the Patuxent Patu on Maryland's Western Shore. After contrary winds forced his vessels into the shallow St. Leonard Creek, a number of shallow-draft British warships and auxiliaries blocked their exit. On June 10, Barney counterattacked but failed to break the blockade.

The Americans planned a joint operation for a second attempt to free Barney's flotilla. Secretary of War Armstrong sent Colonel Wadsworth to command the land forces. These consisted of Colonel Carberry's understrength 36th U.S. Infantry; several companies of the 38th U.S. Infantry; two 18-pounder long guns and their crews; and a detachment of three 12-pounder field guns commanded by Lt. Thomas Harrison. Secretary Jones augmented the ground forces with one hundred ten marines with three light 12-pounders under the command of Capt. Samuel Miller from the Washington Navy Yard.

As Wadsworth and Barney continued their planning, British Capt. Robert Barrie maintained the blockade and sent barges carrying troops to raid farms and plantations throughout the region. On June 11, members of the 45th Maryland Regiment fired on British raiders near Hallowing Point in Calvert County. In keeping with Admiral Cockburn's standing order, Barrie deployed one hundred seventy marines to burn the farm of Capt. John Broome of the 31st Maryland Regiment.

Ship rating

During the august age of sail from the 17th to the 19th centuries, the Royal Navy classified its warships according to the rating system. This system denoted fighting vessels according to six "rates," in descending order of size, established by the number of gun decks, and the number of guns carried, plus factors such as tonnage, complement and the role which the ships played tactically. The First, Second and Third Rates were the biggest and most formidable, regarded as the "ships-of-the-line," i.e. those capable of taking a place in the "line of battle" formation in ship vs ship engagements. First and Second Rates were three-deckers, the First Rate having 100+ guns (these vessels often served as flagships) while the Second Rate had 90–98 guns. The Third Rate ships had two decks with 64–80 guns. Classified below the ships-of-the-line, the Fourth Rate also had two decks, but was armed with 50–60 guns, while the Fifth Rate had but a single gundeck and 32–40 guns. Sixth Rate vessels were smaller frigates of 22–28 guns. Although the First–Third Rate vessels were certainly the most powerful and impressive of the fleet, the Fourth–Sixth Rates were the most numerous and busy, offering a useful balance between firepower, maneuverability, and speed. Beneath the six classes of fighting vessel was also a whole other dimension of "unrated" vessels, which included sloops, bomb ships, gunboats and cutters.

The 1814 Campaign Begins

▲ These modern-day re-enactors demonstrate British Royal Artillery troops in action, firing a 6-pounder field cannon, a piece commonly used in the War of 1812. The individual on the left is just applying a lit match to the cannon's touchhole. (Detail Heritage/Alamy Stock Photo)

After raiding Benedict, Maryland, on June 15, the British penetrated upriver to Lower Marlboro, dispersed the local militia without a fight, and burned more than twenty-five hundred hogsheads of tobacco. On June 18, Colonel Carberry led his regulars in an effort to stop the raids, but failed to force an engagement.

When the British appeared off Nottingham, Maryland, on June 19, Secretary Armstrong sent Maj. George Peter—in command of about two hundred eighty men of the District of Columbia militia, including an infantry company, some dragoons, an artillery company with six field pieces, and a rifle company—to meet them. The dragoons leading the column saw smoke and believed the town had already been burned. However, a detachment of regulars from the 36th U.S. Infantry, supported by Lieutenant Harrison's artillery, had prevented the British from capturing the town. The following day, Peter's force surprised a British raiding party near Benedict and captured several prisoners.

On June 20, Barney received an order from Jones to haul what military materiel he could salvage to Washington and destroy the flotilla. Before he could complete preparations to execute the order, Wadsworth convinced the Secretary to countermand his order, suggesting that he could drive the blockaders away with artillery long enough for the flotilla to escape. A detachment of flotillamen, commanded by Sailing Master John Geoghegan, joined the soldiers to build an artillery emplacement under the cover of darkness. Despite some early disagreement on where to dig, the Americans completed an earthen battery, with a furnace to heat shot and two powerful 18-pounders, on a bluff at the mouth of St. Leonard Creek. Wadsworth positioned himself here. Miller and Harrison positioned their field pieces on the high ground facing the Patuxent farther upriver, with regulars and marines in support. Fire from Wadsworth's guns would signal the attack.

At dawn on June 26, the U.S. artillery opened fire on two British warships, as Barney's barges closed and added their guns. Capt. Thomas Brown of H.M.S. *Loire*, commanding in Barrie's absence, saw that his ships' guns could not silence the land batteries. He ordered his ships to shift their fire to the barges, but soon signaled a withdrawal, allowing Barney's force to escape the creek and head up the Patuxent after suffering six killed and four wounded. As the naval action continued, the British attempted to outflank the batteries by landing marines, supported by a rocket boat. Meanwhile, Miller's 12-pounders had exhausted their supply of shot, while the light field guns had also ceased firing. Wadsworth ordered a detachment toward the shoreline to oppose the landing. When the 36th U.S. Infantry started moving to reposition, however, the inexperienced 38th U.S. Infantry, having earlier received directions to follow the 36th wherever it went, followed suit. Miller, ignorant of Wadsworth's orders, thought the army was retreating and joined the movement as well. Left without support, Wadsworth ordered his guns spiked and rode to the rear to try to rally his confused men.

Wadsworth was initially dissatisfied with the performance of the troops under his command, and noted in his report that "the fact is, the infantry and light artillery decided upon a retreat without my orders before they lost a single man killed or wounded." However, "in justice to the infantry," he added, "[I] acknowledge that they did not take to flight, but quitted the ground in perfect order." The colonel then brought them back toward their original positions, but the British had already retired. Capt. Thomas Carberry then led his company of the 36th U.S. Infantry back to the abandoned battery and retrieved the guns, equipment, and five wounded men left behind during the retreat.

The flotilla's escape from St. Leonard Creek left the town of St. Leonard uncovered. Some men returned to recover any military stores worth saving and to scuttle two gunboats that Barney had left behind. British forces ascended the creek on July 2, and after a brief skirmish, laid waste to the town, sparing only the local physician's house at which some wounded were treated. Near nightfall, loaded with hogsheads of tobacco and other plunder, the British retreated to the safety of their ships.

Meanwhile, learning from spies in Europe that the British were preparing to send an infantry division to the Chesapeake, President James Madison created the 10th Military District to encompass Virginia north of the Rappahannock River, the District of Columbia, and the entire state of Maryland. Over Armstrong's objection, Madison appointed Brig. Gen. William H. Winder to the command. Winder, defeated and captured at the battle of Stony Creek, Upper Canada, the year before, had recently been exchanged in a prisoner swap. He owed his selection as commander of the 10th Military District to the fact that he was the nephew of the Maryland Governor, and Madison hoped his appointment would help garner Federalist support for the war in the state.

General Winder discovered the region was unprepared. In a July 9 letter to Secretary of War Armstrong, he lamented that at best his district had only about one thousand regulars, which included artillerymen in fixed fortifications. The understrength and partially trained 36th and 38th U.S. Infantry constituted his only mobile force, which left most of the burden on militia. He further reminded the Secretary that the British, having conducted extensive reconnaissance for over a year, could land almost anywhere with little to no warning.

▲ President James Madison was the fourth President of the United States, holding the office during the turbulent years of 1809 to 1817. (White House Historical Association)

As Admiral Cochrane pondered his next move, Cockburn suggested that landing an army at Benedict, Maryland, would simultaneously threaten Washington, Annapolis, and Baltimore, thus fixing the militia in their local areas and allowing the British to deal with American defenses piecemeal. In June, Lt. Gen. Sir George Prevost, Governor General and Commander in Chief of British Forces in North America, wrote to Cochrane that U.S. forces had raided the town of Port Dover in Upper Canada the previous month and destroyed private property as well as military targets. Cochrane took the news as an order to retaliate in kind, although Cockburn had essentially been doing so, and directed the indiscriminate destruction of farms and towns.

After leaving a few ships on the Patuxent, Admiral Cockburn divided the rest of his force into two squadrons. One sailed toward Baltimore, while he personally led the other to the mouth of the Potomac. Appearing in three major thoroughfares at once, Cockburn kept Winder guessing where the British would make their main effort. Meanwhile, he launched small raids up and down the coast. Along

The Chesapeake Campaign, 1813–14

Maryland's Western Shore, British troops burned the villages of Huntingtown and Prince Frederick (county seat of Calvert County) after dispersing the local militia without much of a fight. In mid-July, Cockburn turned his attention to Virginia's Northern Neck, burning Nomini Church. The following month, the British admiral sent twenty barges up the Yeocomico River. Elements of the 47th Virginia Regiment, under the command of Capt. William Henderson, attacked and killed a number of the Royal Marines as they came ashore on August 3, but ran low on ammunition and retreated. The British then burned and pillaged Henderson's plantation as well as other farms with fervor. According to Brig. Gen. John P. Hungerford, commanding officer of the 14th Virginia Brigade, hundreds of slaves flocked to the British after the redcoats laid waste to the village of Kinsale. On August 6, Cockburn pushed up Virginia's Coan River, where the Lancaster County militia put up a stout fight before they withdrew. The raiders again burned farms, confiscated supplies, and seized three schooners. Making nine raids in twenty-five days, the British seemed to be everywhere at once.

▲ William H. Winder, by Charles Balthazar Julien Févret de Saint-Mémin. (Library of Congress)

When it appeared that Annapolis was the next British target, Winder ordered the 36th and 38th U.S. Infantry to establish a new camp on the South River near the Maryland capital, with Brig. Gen. Stephen West's Prince George's County Militia replacing the regulars at Nottingham, Maryland. While Winder was constantly in motion, he seemed to focus entirely on details better left to staff officers, rather than planning a coherent defense of the entire region. Militia units responded to alarms, many of which proved unfounded, while the two regular battalions remained near Annapolis. Cockburn's raids had confused Winder exactly as the British had hoped. Militia commanders rarely mustered enough force to oppose even minor incursions, and vulnerable towns demanded that their soldiers remain at home.

On August 14, Cochrane's flagship, H.M.S. *Tonnant*, rendezvoused with Cockburn's advance squadron at the mouth of the Potomac River. Two days later, transports carrying Maj. Gen. Robert Ross and the veteran 4th, 21st, 44th, and 85th Regiments of Foot and a detachment of the Royal Artillery arrived from Europe. Added to the Royal Marine battalions with the fleet, Cochrane now had a substantial land force. Cockburn advocated striking Washington, but Cochrane and Ross doubted the wisdom of such a move, reasoning that the distance of the capital city from the proposed landing point would make their ground force too vulnerable.

The 1814 Campaign Begins

Cockburn eventually won the argument, however, by pointing out that small British forces had easily dispersed the militia in the past. As a compromise, they decided to deal with Barney's flotilla at Nottingham, clearing any militia from the banks of the Patuxent River, before making a final decision about striking Washington.

At 0200 on August 19, Ross' army began an unopposed landing at Benedict, and all were ashore the following day. Ross took his time getting his men on the road to Nottingham, which they reached late on the twenty-first. Cockburn led the naval advance up the Patuxent, the barges and boats moving parallel to Ross' column. Barney had moved his flotilla above the bend in the river at Pig Point, as far as

▶ Major General Robert Ross is most famous for his commanding role in the burning of Washington in August 1814. He was a forceful and effective military leader, his propulsive career only arrested by a sharpshooter's bullet. (PD)

the increasingly narrow and shallow Patuxent allowed. With the flotilla doomed, Barney marched with most of his men toward Washington to join forces with Winder. He left Lt. Solomon Frazier in command of one hundred twenty men with orders to burn their boats if the British approached. Barney also ordered Captain Miller to bring his company and the three 12-pounders to join him on the road from Upper Marlboro (see Map 4).

On the morning of August 22, Cockburn's barges rounded Pig Point and spotted the flotilla. He wrote:

> I landed the marines under Captain Robyns on the left bank of the river, and directed him to march round and attack, on the land side. ... I plainly discovered Commodore Barney's broad pendant in the headmost vessel, a large sloop [*Scorpion*], and the remainder of the flotilla extending in a line astern of her. Our boats now advanced ... but on nearing them, we observed the sloop ... to be on fire, and she soon afterwards blew up. I now saw clearly that they were all abandoned, and on fire, with trains to their magazines; out of the seventeen vessels ... sixteen were in quick succession blown to atoms, and the seventeenth ... we captured.

▼ An artifact conservator at Naval History and Heritage Command inspects a piece of pottery recovered from the wreck of the sloop-of-war U.S.S. *Scorpion*, scuttled in the Patuxent River during the War of 1812. (U.S. Navy photo by Mass Communication Specialist 2nd Class Kenneth G. Takada/Released)

On the same day, Secretary of the Navy Jones notified Master Commandant John O. Creighton, commanding Washington's naval defenses, that six British ships were "ascending the Potomac" and had passed Kettle Bottom Shoals. Admiral Cochrane had ordered these ships to act in support of the main effort by Ross, or to stand ready to evacuate the troops should their line of retreat be cut. Commanded by Capt. James A. Gordon, the squadron included two frigates, three bomb vessels, and a rocket-firing ship, which the British believed adequate to reduce Fort Washington and deal with any American gunboats.

By the afternoon of August 22, Ross' infantry occupied Upper Marlboro, county seat of Prince George's County, as Winder concentrated his forces at Long Old Fields—about eight miles from Washington. Cochrane congratulated Cockburn on the destruction of Barney's flotilla, which he believed was the primary goal of the

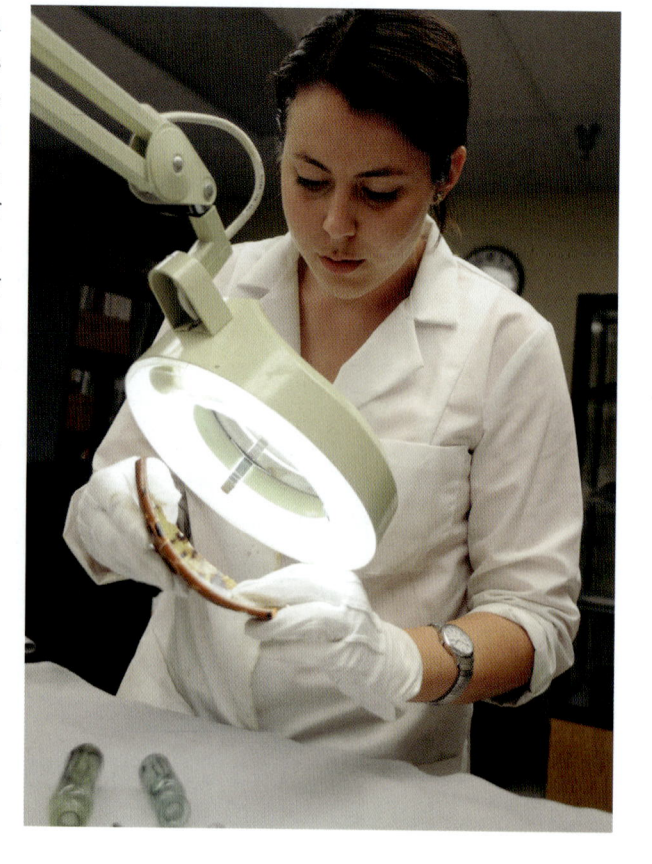

APPROACH TO WASHINGTON
August 19–24, 1814

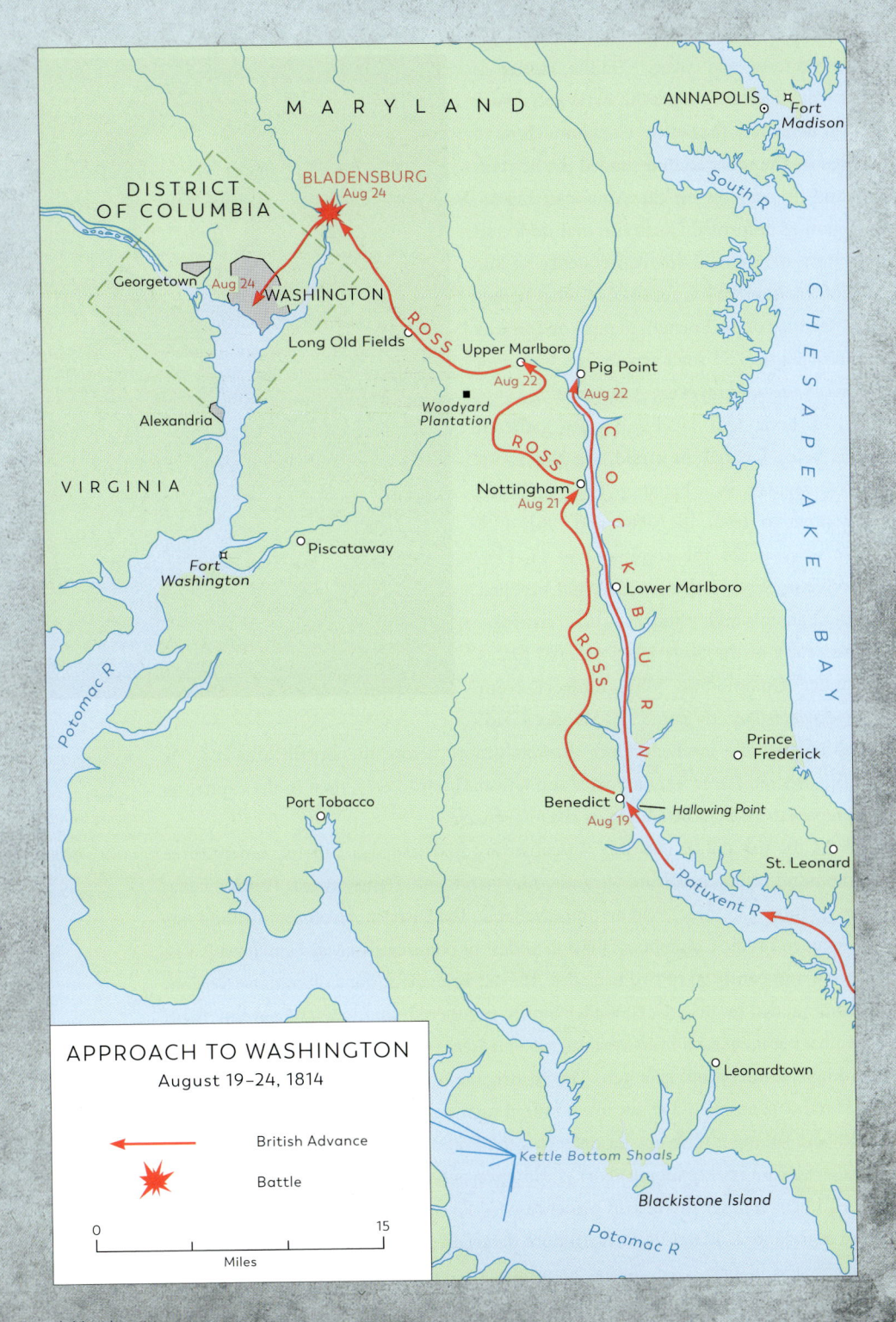

← British Advance

✸ Battle

0 — 15 Miles

Map 4

expedition, and wrote: "[T]he matter is ended, [and] the sooner the Army get[s] back [to Benedict], the better." Cockburn chose to ignore the order and persuaded the hesitant Ross to advance on the American capital. He then informed Cochrane that he found "Ross determined (in consequence of the Information he has received & what he has Observed of the Enemy), to push on towards Washington ... I shall accompany him & of course afford him every Assistance."

At Long Old Fields, Winder gathered as much force as he could. He had about 330 regulars in a battalion that combined companies from the 36th and 38th U.S. Infantry under the command of Lt. Col. William Scott. Barney added 400 beached flotillamen and Miller's 103 marines. Secretary of the Navy Jones ordered forces under Commodore John Rodgers from Delaware Bay to come to Winder's aid, although none reached closer than Baltimore before the British attacked. He also ordered Capts. David Porter and Oliver Hazard Perry, then in the capital, to prepare to assist in defending its river approach.

As for the militia, on July 4 Armstrong had issued a call for ninety-three thousand militiamen from Virginia, Maryland, and Pennsylvania. Pennsylvania, reorganizing its forces, had no units available. The District of Columbia militia was organized as the Columbian Division under the command of Maj. Gen. John P. Van Ness, and consisted of two brigades. The 1st Brigade of the Columbian Division, commanded by Brig. Gen. Walter Smith, numbered one thousand seventy men, with a regiment each from Washington and Georgetown, and two companies each of light artillery and riflemen. The 2d Brigade of the Columbian Division from Alexandria numbered about five hundred men under the command of Brig. Gen. Robert Young. It took up station across the Potomac near Piscataway, Maryland, where it could either support Fort Washington or threaten the rear of Ross' column.

To help counter the British presence near Washington, General Samuel Smith of Maryland's 3d Division at Baltimore detached a 1,300-man brigade under the command of Brig. Gen. Tobias Stansbury to Winder on August 20. Stansbury arrived at Bladensburg, Maryland, close to the border with the District of Columbia, two days later with one battalion each from the 1st and 2d Maryland

▲ Commodore John Rodgers was a true fighting leader, but also a perceptive diplomat, one who served under a total of six presidents during his military career. (National Gallery of Art/PD)

Regiments under the command of Lt. Cols. John Ragan and John H. Schutz, respectively, and began to build earthworks. Joining them on August 23 were Lt. Col. Joseph Sterrett's 5th Regiment, Maryland Volunteer Infantry; Maj. William Pinckney's 1st Maryland Rifle Battalion; and Capts. Joseph Meyer's American and Richard Magruder's Franklin Artillery Companies, each with three 6-pounders. John Pendleton Kennedy, an 18-year-old private in Sterrett's regiment, wrote: "This was a real army marching to a real war. The enemy, we knew, was in full career and we had the certainty of meeting him in a few days."

Late on August 22, Winder ordered General Walter Smith to move his 1st Columbian Brigade and Colonel Scott's composite battalion toward the Woodyard on the road to Upper Marlboro. Meanwhile, Major Peter led a detachment of militia on reconnaissance to determine British intentions. The 60th Virginia Regiment, under Col. George Minor, arrived from Falls Church, but many of the men lacked powder or flints. After sleeping on the floor of the House of Representatives on the night of the twenty-third, they reported to the arsenal at Greenleaf Point, where Colonel Carberry, formerly of the 36th U.S. Infantry, supplied the items.

While the British remained at Upper Marlboro on the morning of August 23, Armstrong convinced the President that since the British possessed no cavalry or artillery, they could not storm the city. Both he and General Winder firmly believed that Annapolis was the most likely British objective. By 1400, however, Ross revealed his intentions. After leaving a rear guard at Upper Marlboro, the army

▼ Re-enactors form ranks during their depiction of the battle of Bladensburg. Although the Revolutionary War taught the value of light skirmishing forces, the War of 1812 was still often fought with volley fire from ordered ranks. (S L O W K I N G/GFDL v1.2; https://www.gnu.org/licenses/old-licenses/fdl-1.2.html)

marched toward Washington. The 1st, or Light Brigade, under the command of Col. William Thornton, comprised the veteran 85th Regiment of Foot and the light infantry companies from all four regiments, plus one company each of British and colonial marines. The 2d Brigade, commanded by Col. Arthur Brooke, included the 4th and 44th Regiments of Foot. The 3d Brigade of Col. William Patterson was composed of the 21st Foot and the 2d Battalion of Royal Marines. They were followed by detachments of sailors, shipboard marines, and artillery.

The advance guard easily forced Major Peter's detachment to retire and then conducted some countermarches to confuse the Americans. Before Peter's men arrived at Long Old Fields, Secretary of State Monroe, who fancied himself as more of a military man than a diplomat, wrote to Madison: "General Winder proposes to retire. ... The enemies are in full march to Washington. Have the materials prepared to destroy the bridges. P.S.—You had better remove the records."

Just before nightfall, General Winder ordered his forces at Long Old Fields to retreat across the Eastern Branch of the Potomac (now called the Anacostia River), and told Stansbury to form a defensive line on the river's right bank at Bladensburg. The Eastern Branch was too deep to ford between Bladensburg and its confluence

Royal Marines

With their origins dating back to the 17th century, the Royal Marines were already a small but superior naval fighting force by the outbreak of the War of 1812. Its manpower had reached 31,400 men, albeit scattered across a wide range of British global deployments. Royal Marines were to be found wherever the British sent their major warships. They formed part of the complement aboard Royal Navy men-of-war: 29 marines were aboard a frigate, swelling to 104 on a First-Rate ship of the line.

The marines were a primarily used as naval infantry. In ship-versus-ship actions, they provided accurate musket fire and operated cannon, and were in the thick of the action in boarding parties. But they also served on land, conducting amphibious landings as a prelude to coastal raids or participating in full-blown expeditionary campaigns. During the Chesapeake campaign, their ranks were also swollen by the recruitment of escaped slaves; this new source of personnel formed the 2d Corps of Colonial Marines, established by Alexander Cochrane. Prominent battles fought by the Royal Marines and the Colonial Marines during the War of 1812 included Bladensburg and the assault on Washington.

▲ The "Undaunted in Battle," a memorial to the battle of Bladensburg, was designed and sculpted by Joanna Blake and was dedicated at Bladensburg, Maryland, on August 23, 2014. The monument depicts a wounded Commodore Joshua Barney, commander of the Chesapeake Flotilla, Charles Ball, a freed slave and flotilla man, and an unnamed Marine. (U.S.M.C.)

with the Potomac. Ross had no means to build bridges, so the Americans could easily prevent him from entering Washington south of Bladensburg either by defending or destroying the two bridges that spanned the lower reaches of the Eastern Branch. A third bridge, however, existed at Bladensburg itself, just above the head of navigation. Here, the Eastern Branch narrowed and even became fordable in places. Winder was convinced that an advance toward Washington would come that way.

As panic struck Washington, clerks loaded government records for shipment to safety. When he realized that no one had carried out his orders to destroy the two lower bridges over the Eastern Branch, Winder had the commandant of the Washington Navy Yard, Capt. Thomas Tingey, supply the necessary boats and powder, with Barney's men protecting them until the job was complete. He then ordered the East Capitol Bridge set on fire.

49

The Battle of Bladensburg, August 24, 1814

As the Americans fell back to Bladensburg, Admiral Cochrane directed his subordinates to return to Benedict. Arguing that "we must go on," Cockburn convinced Ross to disregard Cochrane's order, and on the morning of August 24, the British resumed marching toward Washington. Meanwhile, after some hesitation as to where best to establish his main defensive line, Winder deployed his forces.

He ordered the 1st Columbian Brigade, Scott's regulars, and Lt. Col. Jacint Laval's 140-man squadron of the 1st U.S. Dragoons to march to Bladensburg immediately. Barney, left behind at the site of the lower bridges, requested and received the president's permission to follow with his brigade. Madison and his entourage went out as well, nearly riding into the path of the British advance guard before observant vedettes redirected them to a place of relative safety. As the troops arrived, Winder had little time to sort out and position units, resulting in a haphazard defense.

Stansbury had placed the six 6-pounders of his two artillery companies in an earthen battery position—called a barbette—about 350 yards from the Bladensburg Bridge, and deployed Pickney's riflemen in the brush along the river's western bank. On orders from Winder, he posted the rest of his brigade in a second line to cover the junction on the Georgetown Pike, where the Washington Pike forked toward the capital. Stansbury arrayed Ragan's and Schutz's battalions on line in an orchard with Sterrett's in support. When the Columbian Brigade arrived, Wadsworth positioned one of its artillery companies, with three 6-pounders, on the Georgetown Pike to the left of Stansbury's second line, and Winder sent Capt. John Doughty's Navy Yard Rifles to Pickney's left flank. Laval's dragoons, along with several militia cavalry units, took a position behind and to the left of Stansbury's

The Battle of Bladensburg, August 24, 1814

line. Monroe suggested that the horsemen occupy a deep ravine, but the ground proved so low that the troopers could see nothing to their front. He then without consulting either Stansbury or Winder ordered Schutz and Ragan to move their troops five hundred yards to the rear, where they could support neither Sterrett nor the skirmishers. The move essentially left the forward deployed artillery companies and riflemen without infantry support to oppose an attack. Before Stansbury could correct the error, British units appeared outside of Bladensburg.

Winder hurriedly formed a third defensive line on high ground just beyond where Turncliff Bridge crossed the stream at the bottom of the ravine. Just north, or left, of the road, he positioned Walter Smith's Columbian Brigade with Scott's regulars extending to the left, supported by Major Peter's six light field guns. Capt. John Stull's District of Columbia Rifles and Capt. John Davidson's Union Rifles took up positions forward of this line to dominate the ravine. As soon as Barney's command arrived, he placed his heavy guns on the Washington Pike to the right of Smith's brigade, and extended to the right with sailors acting as infantry and Miller's marines. Finally, Col. William Beall's composite brigade of eight hundred men drawn from three Maryland regiments arrived from Annapolis just ahead of the British advance and took position on a hill to Miller's right (Map 5). Winder, however, never told Smith, Barney, or Beall what he expected them to accomplish. By noon, the hastily assembled defenders numbered about seven thousand, mostly inadequately trained militia.

▲ Joshua Barney (1759–1818) served not only the Continental Navy and U.S. Navy, he also served for six years (1796–1802) as a captain in the French Navy. (National Museum of the U.S. Navy)

The British Army consisted of about four thousand veterans. The Light Brigade arrived first. On seeing the Americans across the river, Lt. George Gleig of the 85th Foot described that the Americans "were on a bare hill, their battle line very awkward in appearance, drawn three ranks deep ... [and more] like a crowd of spectators" than soldiers. He noted that "they were sufficiently armed but wretchedly equipped." Ross decided to attack immediately and ordered Colonel Thornton to advance the Light Brigade across the bridge without waiting for the 2d and 3d Brigades.

51

The Chesapeake Campaign, 1813–14

◀ This artwork by the great American painter Colonel Charles Waterhouse (1924–2013) depicts U.S. marines manning their guns at Bladensburg, Maryland, in defense of Washington, D.C. against the British on August 24, 1814. (Colonel Charles Waterhouse/ U.S.M.C. Art Collection)

When the Americans near the bridge noticed the 85th Foot preparing to attack, they opened fire with artillery. To minimize casualties, Thornton ordered his men to form behind the cover of nearby Lowndes Hill, prompting the Americans to cheer believing the British were retreating. The 85th Foot re-formed and advanced. Maryland militia Pvt. Henry Fulford observed that "their men moved like clockwork; the instant a part of a platoon was cut down it was filled up by the men in the rear without the least noise and confusion whatever, so as to present always a solid column to the mouths of our cannon." At the same time, Ross had his Royal Marine Artillery fire their Congreve rockets at the American first line.

Thornton, mounted on his horse and waving his sword, led his men across the bridge. They reached the far side, fanned out to secure the bridgehead, and drove the Americans from the riverbank. The severely wounded Pinckney ordered his riflemen to withdraw, and despite the quickness of the British advance, the artillerymen brought most of their guns. Thornton deployed his men in open order and urged them forward in a rush toward the second American line. Stansbury's battalions withstood the initial onslaught and forced the British back toward the riverbank. Stansbury ordered Sterrett's 5th Maryland, with remnants of the rifle battalion, to counterattack the Light Brigade as it re-formed in the orchard. Sterrett's men advanced and held their own, trading volleys with the British, until Thornton extended his line to overlap their flanks. Meanwhile, Ross ordered Colonel Brooke to advance the 2d Brigade against the flanks of the American second line battalions as rocket fire concentrated on the militiamen.

The 4th Foot crossed the bridge and pressed Stansbury's right flank as the 44th Foot forded upstream and attacked Sterrett's left. Seeing the 5th Maryland pressed

The Battle of Bladensburg, August 24, 1814

on three sides, Winder ordered a withdrawal. Thornton's redcoats then resumed their advance, with Brooke's 4th and 44th Foot threatening the left and right flanks, respectively, of what remained of Stansbury's line. Unnerved by the rocket fire, many of Schutz's and Ragan's men were unable to resist further. They managed two volleys and then began to retire. Although the withdrawal started in good order, it soon became a rout. Colonel Ragan attempted to rally his troops, but was injured, thrown from his horse, and taken prisoner. As British forces advanced on the retreating 5th Maryland, it too dissolved.

Winder had expected the units from the first and second lines to rally behind the third line, but his orders were unclear, and instead the withdrawing troops raced down the Georgetown Pike toward Washington and away from the battle. As the fleeing infantry passed the dragoons, a number of the horsemen joined

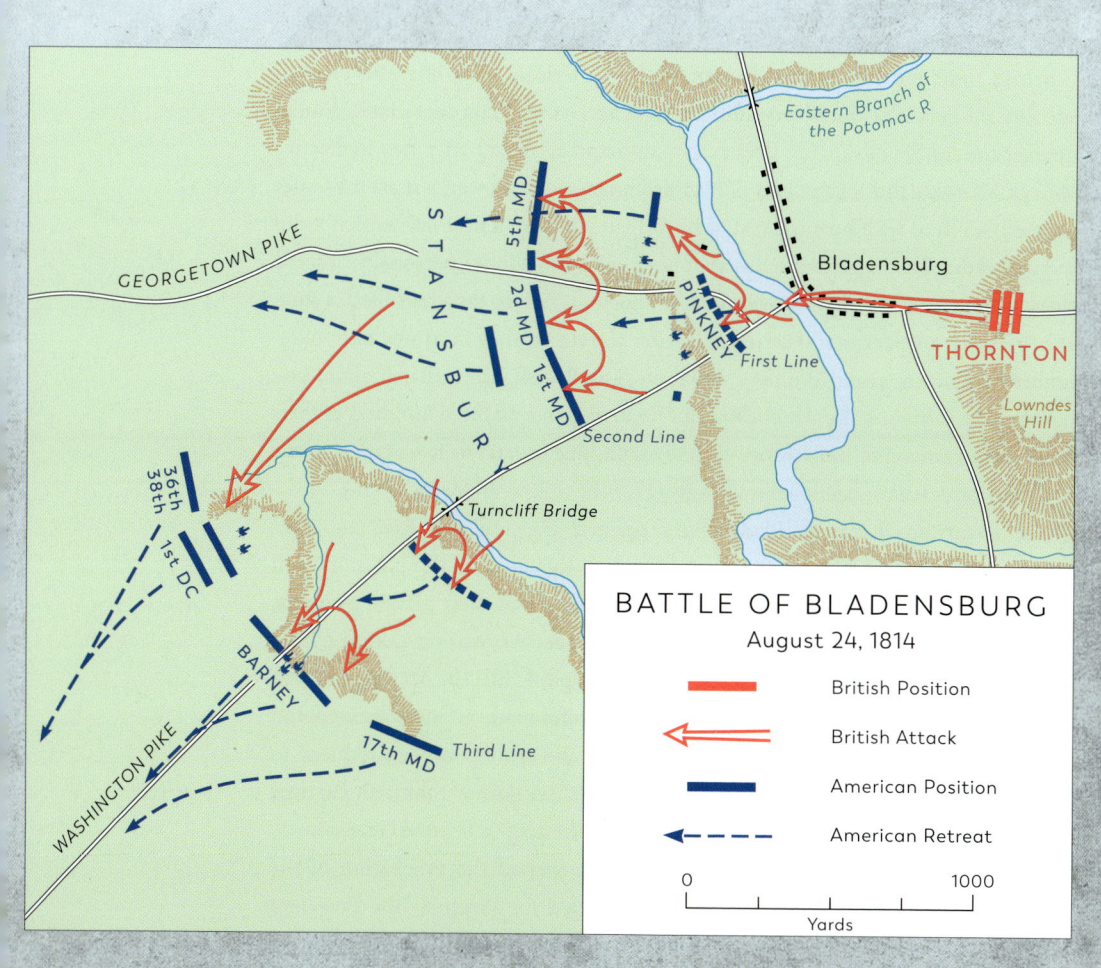

▲ Map 5

the retreat. After an out-of-control artillery wagon hit and injured him, Laval led his remaining troopers toward Georgetown. The president witnessed the debacle unfold. By 1400, he sullenly made his way back to Washington to prepare to evacuate the government.

After forcing the District of Columbia militiamen guarding Turncliff Bridge to scatter, Ross' men encountered stiffer resistance. Fire from Barney's five guns in the road halted their advance, and Peter's 6-pounders hammered the British as well. Ross therefore ordered a wider flanking movement. Beall's militia fired two ineffective volleys and then retreated, leaving the American right flank exposed. Upon seeing this, Miller led the sailors and marines in a counterattack that briefly checked the threat to the American artillery. With most artillery ammunition expended, civilian drivers fleeing, and enemy troops dangerously near, Barney ordered his sailors and marines to spike their guns and to retreat as best they could. The British captured Barney and Miller, both wounded, and a number of their men before they could evacuate their position.

British units moving against the left of the American third line also enjoyed success. The nervous Columbian militiamen of Col. George Magruder's 1st Regiment opened fire on the advancing British too soon and retreated after two ineffective volleys. Knowing that a large part of his third line was giving way, a shaken Winder ordered Smith to withdraw the rest of his brigade to form a new line, which it did in good order. The regulars remained in position until Winder personally ordered them to join Smith's brigade, over Scott's objection, before they had fired a shot. When Peter's artillerymen received the order to retreat, they fired one last volley, limbered their guns, and skillfully withdrew. The British had inflicted about one hundred casualties on the Americans, but incurred close to three hundred of their own. Losses among officers were especially high, due in part to Ross ordering the Light Brigade's hasty assault without waiting for the follow-on forces.

The American defeat at Bladensburg opened the way for Ross to enter Washington. Most of Winder's army fled through the city and did not stop until reaching Georgetown. Disheartened and concerned about their private property, many militiamen left the ranks and returned home. Armstrong, Monroe, and Winder debated whether to make a last stand on Capitol Hill. The Secretary of War suggested that the stout limestone walls of the Capitol made an ideal strongpoint, but Monroe and especially Winder believed that the army had been reduced to a point at which it could not offer a credible defense. Rather than risk capture, General Winder recommended that they retreat to the heights beyond Georgetown. Meanwhile, President Madison's wife, Dolley, supervised the evacuation of the executive mansion—or White House—and departed for Virginia. The President with some key aides fled first to Virginia then to Montgomery Court House (now Rockville), Maryland.

The Battle of Bladensburg, August 24, 1814

After allowing his exhausted, albeit victorious, troops a short rest, Ross led the 3d Brigade into the city late on the twenty-fourth. At about sunset, British soldiers set the House of Representatives, Senate, and the Library of Congress ablaze. Shots fired from the vicinity of Robert Sweall's house killed one and wounded three British soldiers, and shot Ross' horse from under him. Unable to find those responsible, Ross ordered the house burned. Meanwhile, Captain Tingey and the last clerks and sailors evacuated the Navy Yard after demolishing it and setting the nearly completed frigate *Columbia* and sloop-of-war *Argus* on fire to prevent their capture. Admiral Cockburn ordered the President's mansion and the nearby Treasury building looted and burned. The buildings were fully engulfed in flames in a short time, but a hard rain limited much of the damage. With their objective

▶ Modern-day U.S. sailors demonstrate some of the naval gunnery skills of their forebears during the War of 1812. Here one of the sailors adjusts the elevation with a wooden beam. (STS2 [SS] Thomas Rooney/U.S. Navy)

The Chesapeake Campaign, 1813–14

◀ Capture and burning of Washington by the British, in 1814. (Library of Congress)

accomplished, the British troops began their return march to Upper Marlboro late on the twenty-fifth. Back in Benedict by August 29, they loaded aboard their vessels and rejoined the fleet two days later.

Sloop-of-war

The sloop-of-war was a much-used fighting vessel during the age of sail, not least during the War of 1812. The term "sloop-of-war" actually had a somewhat slippery definition, as it could be applied to almost any unrated warship, but they had some unifying characteristics. Depending on the type, they had either two or three masts (in contrast with a civilian sloop, which had a single mast with fore and aft rigging). These ships were called "brig sloops" and "ship sloops" respectively; there was another three-master type called a "Bermuda sloop." All the ships had a single gun deck armed with 10–20 guns, typically a mix of 24- and 12-pounders, but often with smaller calibers and carronades for short-range anti-ship/anti-crew engagements. They had a crew of approximately 120 personnel. Sloops of war could be sizeable—large specimens had displacements of more than 250 tons. They could handle a wide range of roles—convoy escort, blockade operations, coastal patrols, reconnaissance and scouting, commerce raiding, courier and dispatch duties, towing and salvage, amphibious landing support, and more.

The Battle of Bladensburg, August 24, 1814

British raids, August 1814

While Ross and his men returned to their transports, Capt. James Gordon's Potomac River squadron arrived opposite Fort Washington on August 27, just out of range of its batteries. In preparation for a dawn attack, Gordon had his powerful bomb vessels commence firing their heavy mortars. General Winder had earlier ordered the fort's commander, Capt. Samuel T. Dyson, to blow up the magazine, destroy the works, and evacuate the fort if attacked from its landward side. Dyson did not wait. As soon as the first shells fell, he destroyed the fort and fled with his sixty-man garrison. With the fort neutralized, Gordon headed for Alexandria, with its fully stocked warehouses and harbor crowded with merchant vessels.

The mayor and city leaders surrendered the city on August 28, trusting Gordon's promise that he would only seize property of military or commercial value and would not burn or loot the town if he encountered no resistance. After the army returned to the transports, a courier ship brought Gordon orders to rejoin the fleet. The return journey proved more dangerous than the raid. Capt. David Porter of the U.S. Navy had come to Washington with one hundred sailors and marines to man the frigate *Columbia*. With the ship destroyed, Porter joined forces with General Hungerford, who had positioned infantry and field artillery along the riverbank near White House Landing to harass Gordon's ships as they struggled to get back down the river. Nevertheless, all eight British warships and twenty-one heavily laden prizes rejoined the fleet. After the fight, Porter commended "Captain Spencer of the U.S. Artillery late second in command at Fort Washington and now in command of the officers and men ... attached to my command by the War Department—they have given the most unquestionable proof that it was not want of courage on their part which caused the destruction of that Fort."

Two days after the British left Washington, President Madison and most of his cabinet returned to the nation's capital. Recriminations

▼ A time-battered American merchant ship ensign from the War of 1812. This specific hand-sewn artefact was from a merchant brig captured by the British ship H.M.S. *Borer*. (National Maritime Museum, Greenwich/PD)

The Chesapeake Campaign, 1813–14

The Battle of Bladensburg, August 24, 1814

over who was responsible for the Bladensburg debacle followed, and much blame fell on Armstrong. No longer enjoying the President's favor, Armstrong tendered his resignation and went home to New York. Monroe took over, concurrently serving as Secretary of State and Secretary of War.

As the events around Washington transpired toward the end of August, a small British squadron under Capt. Sir Peter Parker appeared off Kent Island. Parker had orders to create a diversion that would keep Eastern Shore militia from reinforcing Baltimore or Washington, and to seize material worth prize money. After burning and looting two farms, Parker learned that two hundred men of the 21st Maryland Regiment, under the command of Revolutionary War veteran Lt. Col. Philip Reed, had gathered near Chestertown. Late on August 30, Parker landed with 125 sailors and marines and raided two farms called Waltham and Chantilly before moving against the militia camp.

Ordering his men to form a line near his campsite and on a slight rise at a clearing called Caulk's Field, Reed prepared to contest the raiders' progress. He arrayed four infantry companies in line, with an artillery company and its five light cannon in the center, facing the

◀ The historic site of Fort Washington Park. The original fort was completed in 1809 and was at first named Fort Warburton. The fort was destroyed by its own garrison to avoid capture or reduction by the British. (Ken Lund/CC BY-SA 2.0)

Cannon shot

In both naval and land warfare, smoothbore cannon could fire a bloody spectrum of ammunition types, each intended to deliver a specific effect on human or material targets. By far the most common was round shot, a solid sphere made from soft iron (hard iron was too brittle to withstand the compression of firing). In naval warfare, this was used to penetrate hulls and smash spars and masts; in land engagements, it scythed through ranks of infantry and blew open fortifications. In naval clashes it could also be heated until glowing; this "hot shot" was used to cause onboard fires. Additional destruction to an enemy ship and its personnel could be delivered via chain shot (two metal spheres connected by a length of chain) or bar-shot (two metal spheres connected by a solid iron bar), both of which were primarily designed to slash down rigging and sail with dreadful efficiency. For pure anti-personnel effects, "grapeshot" was an indiscriminate option. Although the specific designs varied, the essence was a canvas bag containing multiple iron balls, each weighing anywhere from 8oz to 4lb; the name "grapeshot" came from the ammunition's similarity to a bunch of grapes. When fired, the canvas bag burst and the iron balls were delivered rather like a massively augmented shotgun blast over hundreds of yards, although its maximum effect was at short range against tight ranks of enemy troops.

open field. In a wood just forward of the clearing, Reed deployed a company of riflemen under the command of Capt. Simon Wickes to act as skirmishers. With the ambient illumination of a full moon and guided by a captured slave, Parker's force approached the American line. When the column was within seventy paces, Wickes opened fire. Parker's men immediately deployed into battle formation and drove the riflemen back toward the right of Reed's main line. Thinking that the militia were retreating, the British surged ahead to exploit their success. Instead of being routed, the Americans repulsed the British advance with blasts of grapeshot and musketry.

Parker re-formed his men and attempted to turn Reed's left flank, but once again the Marylanders stood firm. The fighting continued for more than an hour until both sides had nearly exhausted their ammunition. A crucial turning point in the fighting came when Parker was struck in the leg. Not believing that the wound was serious, he continued to urge his men forward. A piece of buckshot, however, had nicked his femoral artery and he bled to death. Other British casualties included fourteen dead and twenty-seven wounded, as compared to one dead and three wounded Americans. Defeated, the British returned to their ships to rejoin the fleet.

Meanwhile, back on Maryland's Western Shore, former Maryland governor Robert Bowie, 65-year-old Dr. William Beanes of Academy Hill, and a few other leading citizens of the area outside Washington had rounded up and imprisoned a number of stragglers, wounded, and deserters from Ross' army once it had embarked. One of the detainees escaped and informed the British general—incorrectly—that Dr. Beanes and others were killing the stragglers. Ross sent sixty men back to Upper Marlboro to investigate. Finding that the Americans were holding stragglers and hiding deserters, the British threatened to burn the town unless they were returned. To show that they were serious, they took the doctor and other citizens as prisoners.

Plans and Preparations

In the two weeks that followed, Cochrane vacillated on his next target. He recognized that his primary mission was to draw U.S. forces away from Canada. He wrote to First Lord of the Admiralty Lord Melville on September 3 that once all his troops were re-embarked and fleet united, he intended to sail northward, and possibly raid Rhode Island. After a rest and refit in Nova Scotia, he would then return south in October to strike the Carolinas, Georgia, and ultimately New Orleans, Louisiana. But before he left the Chesapeake, he wanted to take some action against Baltimore.

▼ Samuel Smith, by Rembrandt Peale. (Maryland Historical Society)

Home to hundreds of privateers that had long plagued British commercial shipping, he told Melville that "this town must be laid in ashes." The question was whether to attack now while the Americans were still demoralized following the destruction of their capital or later after he had attacked Rhode Island. Ross preferred to head to Rhode Island first, but Cockburn persuaded both the general and Admiral Cochrane that the time was right to strike Baltimore.

Fortunately for the Americans, they had now had over a year to improve Baltimore's defenses. After the first British vessels had appeared near Baltimore in 1813, Maryland Governor Levin Winder had ordered the local militia commander, General Samuel Smith, to assume responsibility for improving the city's inadequate defenses. An experienced combat veteran, Smith had served as an infantry

Plans and Preparations

officer during the Revolutionary War and had achieved notoriety for the defense of Fort Mifflin in 1777. He had remained active in the militia and had commanded the state's troops called to federal service during the Whiskey Rebellion in 1794. A sitting U.S. senator, Smith proved an excellent choice for the task of enhancing Baltimore's defenses.

His first priority had been to improve Fort McHenry, situated at Whetstone Point, where the Patapsco River split into the Northwest Branch, which led directly into the city's harbor, and the Ferry, or Middle, Branch. Through great effort he had acquired additional cannon from a variety of sources and had Fort McHenry's irascible commander, Maj. Lloyd Beall, replaced with the cooperative veteran Maj. George Armistead. By September 1814, Smith had created a credible defense system for Baltimore's harbor. Fort McHenry's well-trained garrison consisted of sixty regulars of the U.S. Army Corps of Artillery commanded by Capt. Frederick Evans and seventy-five members of the Baltimore Fencibles, a volunteer militia artillery company in federal service commanded by Capt. Joseph H. Nicholson. Across from Fort McHenry on the Northwest Branch was a battery of three 18-pounder guns at Lazaretto Point. Lt. Solomon Frazier commanded the post, which was manned by 45 flotillamen acting as gunners and an additional 114 serving as infantry. The Lazaretto guns not only reinforced Fort McHenry, but also

▼ A model of Fort McHenry in Baltimore, Maryland, shows the star-shaped layout, influenced by European fortress design. Each point of the star acts as an artillery bastion, with interlocking fields of fire. (Ad Meskens/ CC BY-SA 3.0)

The Chesapeake Campaign, 1813–14

covered a log-and-chain boom, backed up by sunken hulks, that obstructed the harbor entrance. Eight barges commanded by Lt. Solomon Rutter, each manned by a crew of 34 flotillamen and armed with an 8- or 12-pounder in the bow, stood behind the line of hulks to further enhance the obstacle. The fact that the Northwest Branch was relatively narrow and too shallow to admit deep-draft warships further strengthened the defense of Baltimore's harbor.

To guard the broader Ferry Branch that offered access to the city from the south, Smith had augmented Fort McHenry with a water battery. The battery, which covered both the main channel as well as the Ferry Branch, consisted of two parallel earthworks along the shoreline. At least fifteen of its thirty-six guns were long-range 42-pounders taken from the wrecked French ship-of-the-line, *L'Eole*, which had run aground off the Virginia Capes in 1806 and had been towed into Baltimore. Commanded by militia Capt. John Berry, the water battery guns were manned by a mixed force consisting of two companies of Maryland volunteer militia artillery—Berry's own Washington Artillery with one hundred men and the Baltimore Independent Artillerists with seventy-five men under the command of Lt. Charles Pennington. Sixty flotillamen commanded by Sailing Master Solomon Rodman and two companies of U.S. Sea Fencibles, at least one hundred ten men in total commanded by Capts. Matthew S. Bunbury and William H. Addison, rounded out the defenders. The Sea Fencibles were a unique corps recruited from unemployed members of the maritime trades by the War Department (the modern-day Department of the Army) to serve in harbor defenses. Four other fortifications to the rear of Fort McHenry completed the water defenses.

Situated on the Ferry Branch about one and three-quarter miles away from Fort McHenry, Fort Babcock (originally called the Sailor's Battery) was a four-foot-

◀ *The Flag is Full of Stars*, by Dale Gallon. (Gallon Historical Art)

Profile:
Sea Fencibles

The origins of the Sea Fencibles lay back in Britain in the early 1790s, when groups of fisherman were formed into a special defense militia to guard English and Irish coastlines from French warships. ("Fencible" was an abbreviated form of the word "defensible.") This rough-hewn naval force was disbanded in 1810, but interest in the model grew in the United States from 1813. A report by the U.S. Senate in June 1813 stated that "there are a large number of seafaring men, who from their hardihood and habits of life, might be very useful in the defense of the seaboard, particularly in the management of the great guns …" On July 26, 1813, the U.S. Congress passed "An act to authorise the raising [of] a Corps of Sea Fencibles."

The Sea Fencibles had a hybrid army/navy administration. The officers were from the U.S. Army, and thus dressed accordingly and received army pay and rations. The other ranks were paid, victualled and equipped by the U.S. Navy. As the Act stated, they served for about one year, and they were largely recruited from the ranks of civilian sailors; each company had an establishment of 107 officers and enlisted men. Although the Sea Fencibles were officially disbanded with the end of the War of 1812, state naval militias survived for the remainder of the century.

▼ Although this certification of enrollment to the Boston Sea Fencibles post-dates the War of 1812, its imagery evokes the distinctive mix of naval, coastal and land warfare that defined the service. (U.S. Marine Corps)

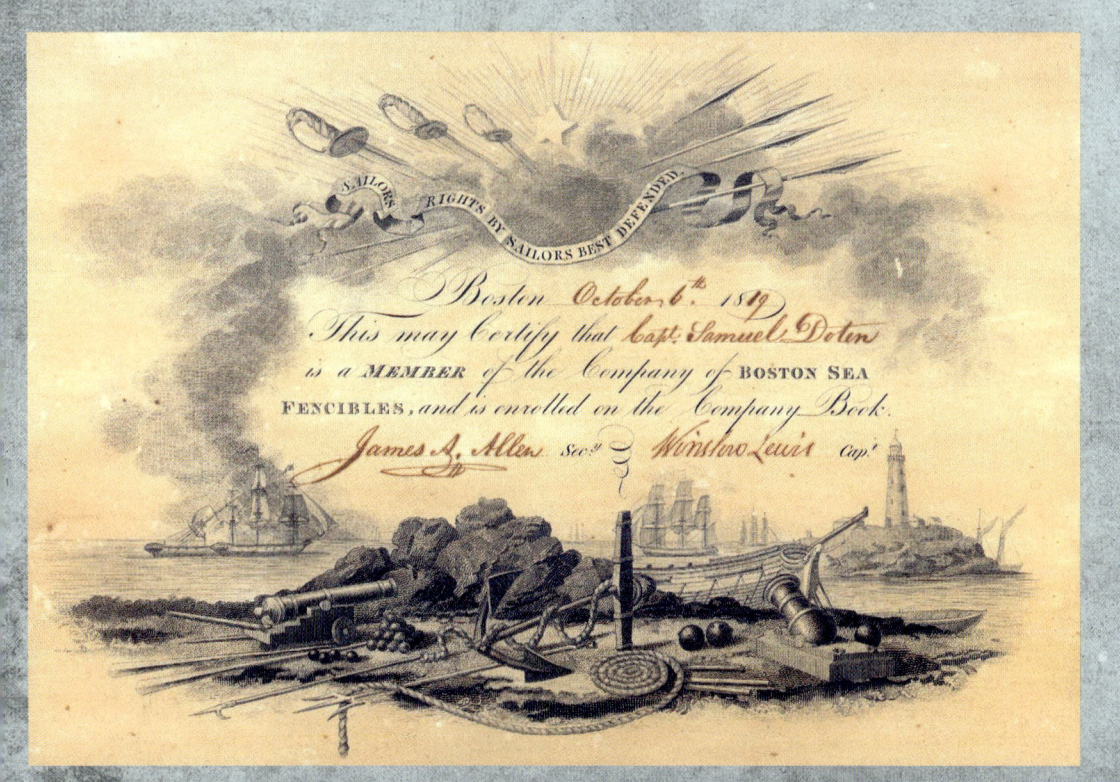

high semicircular earthwork. Fifty-two flotillamen commanded by Sailing Master John A. Webster manned its six 18-pounder naval guns. Two miles west of Fort McHenry and also facing the Ferry Branch was Fort Covington. Originally called Fort Patapsco, it consisted of a fleche or V-shaped battery with a six-foot-deep ditch and ten-foot-high brick wall. Lt. Henry Newcomb commanded the eighty sailors from U.S.S. *Guerriere* who manned its battery of ten to twelve 18-pounder naval guns mounted en barbette, thereby allowing them to fire over the top of the earthen parapet. Guarding the landward approaches to Forts Babcock and Covington was Fort Wood (originally called Fort Lookout), a circular structure with a ten-foot-high "demi-revetted" brick wall with emplacements for ten 18-pounders. A detachment of sailors commanded by Lt. George Budd manned its seven guns. Finally, seamen commanded by Sailing Master Leonard Hall manned a single-gun battery emplaced on Federal Hill overlooking Baltimore harbor. It provided a critical observation post to keep the defenders informed of British naval activity up to twelve miles away.

◀ An impressive sight despite the grainy image—one of the huge flags that flew over Fort McHenry in 1814 is displayed and guarded. It was the sight of the ensign that inspired Francis Scott Key to write the poem "Defence of Fort M'Henry," which would evolve into the U.S. national anthem. (George Henry Preble/PD)

As for Baltimore's land defenses, Smith recognized that the easiest land route into the city was from the east via the Patapsco Neck, with the most likely landing place being at North Point on Old Road Bay, near the point at which the Patapsco River empties into Chesapeake Bay. He had therefore picketed Patapsco Neck and turned Hampstead—or Loundenslager's—Hill, located just east of the city, into a veritable Gibraltar. Studded with batteries and strongpoints, the main American defense line stretched more than one mile long from the Patapsco River shoreline north along the hill to the Belair Road. Smith placed a second line of battery positions on the high ground behind the main line of resistance so that if compelled to retreat, the defenders could continue to fight in depth. Supplemental detached breastworks and batteries guarded approaches from the north and west.

◀ George Armistead, by Rembrandt Peale. (Maryland Historical Society)

▼ Fitted on September 12, 1932 by the "Soroptimist Club" (a volunteer organization established in 1821) of Baltimore, this tree marker remembers Captain William H. Addison for his role in the defense of Fort McHenry in 1814. (Devry Becker Jones/CC0)

The Chesapeake Campaign, 1813–14

Constructing all of these fortifications had taken considerable effort. Fortunately for Smith, he had received the full cooperation of city officials who had formed a Committee of Vigilance and Safety with access to money on easy terms and extensive authority for improving local security. In addition to authorizing Smith to call out the city militia for regular drill and exercises, the committee had required all able-bodied males who did not shoulder muskets to shoulder shovels. Working in shifts every fourth day, every male inhabitant—white and black, free and slave—had been put to work digging entrenchments. They reported at 0600 and toiled until dark. Several militia officers with engineering and construction experience assisted engineer and architect J. Maximilian M. Godefroy in supervising the civilian labor. To facilitate the preparations and relieve the congestion caused by the movement of troops, work parties, and supplies through the city, Smith had a floating bridge built across the harbor.

Plans and Preparations

Expecting an attack at any time, by September 1814 the United States had amassed a considerable force at Baltimore. The federal contribution consisted of the 1st Dragoons; detachments of regulars from the 14th, 36th, and 38th U.S. Infantry; and several hundred sailors and marines, the latter under the command of Commodore Rodgers. The War Department also supplied about fifteen hundred muskets to better arm local militiamen. Maryland provided three militia brigades drawn from around the state. Pennsylvania sent a provisional division of militia under the command of Maj. Gen. Nathaniel Watson, while Virginia contributed a militia division under Maj. Gen. John Pegram. Determined to avoid a repeat of Bladensburg, General Smith had the various units of militia drilling every morning and evening to prepare for the coming battle. When the men were not at drill or on patrol down the Patapsco Neck, they helped dig entrenchments. All totaled, the defenders numbered nearly fourteen thousand, far exceeding the five thousand men the British could put ashore.

Technically, the commander of the 10th Military District, General Winder, should have commanded this impressive force, particularly as he held a federal commission while Smith was only a militia general. The debacle at Bladensburg, however, had damaged General Winder's reputation and several federal and state officials preferred that Smith hold command. Governor Winder deftly resolved the situation when he implied that Smith had become the ranking Army officer when the War Department had called him and his Maryland militia into federal service. When General Winder appealed, acting Secretary of War Monroe assented to Smith's seniority with his silence. Although not pleased, General Winder accepted his subordination.

With the command situation resolved, Smith proceeded to deploy

◀ *Assembly of Troops Before the battle of Baltimore*, by Thomas Ruckle Sr. (Maryland Historical Society)

69

The Chesapeake Campaign, 1813–14

O	GEN ROSS	
A DRAGOONS		D 27 REGIMENT
B 5 REGIMENT		E 39 REGIMENT
C RIFLEMEN		F ARTILLERY

FIRST VIEW of the BATTLE of PA
DEDICATED TO THOSE WHO LOST THEIR FRIENDS IN D
SEPTʳ 12 1814

Plans and Preparations

his forces. He placed the regular infantrymen led by Lt. Col. William Steuart at Fort McHenry. Together with Major Armistead's mixed garrison of regular and militia artillery, Sea Fencibles, and flotillamen, about one thousand troops manned the harbor's principal defensive post. Commodore Rodgers posted some elements of his naval contingent at the Lazaretto Point and Ferry Branch defenses. The rest, mostly from U.S.S. *Guerriere*, took position on Hampstead Hill, with sailors manning the fifteen guns in the five-battery positions closest to the river, and marines behind the breastworks covering the most likely avenue of enemy advance to that sector. That section of the front, running from the Sugar House near the mouth of Harris Creek to the Philadelphia Road, thus became known as Rodgers' Bastion. Smith positioned a provisional brigade commanded by Maryland militia Maj. Bealle Randall behind Rodgers. Randall's men included the reconstituted 1st Maryland Regiment—looking to redeem its reputation tarnished at Bladensburg and now commanded by Capt. Henry Steiner—and a battalion of Pennsylvania volunteer militia riflemen. The companies of Lt. Col. David Harris' 1st Regiment, Maryland Volunteer Artillery, not deployed elsewhere, and Capt. George Stiles' 1st Marine

◀ A contemporary diagram illustrating the movements and events of the battle of Patapsco Neck, September 12, 1814. Careful study shows Ross's horse rearing as its commanding rider is shot. (Library of Congress/PD)

71

Artillery of the Union took position with forty-seven guns emplaced among the three batteries north of the Philadelphia Road. Smith supported them with two Maryland brigades to the rear—Brig. Gen. Thomas Foreman's 1st and Stansbury's 11th—and with detachments behind earthworks east of the York Road at McKim's Hill. Altogether, the main defense line at Hampstead Hill and supporting locations contained ten thousand troops, with sixty-two artillery pieces in mutually supporting batteries and strongpoints.

To ease the tension caused by the subordination of the district commanding general, Smith placed General Winder in charge of the infantry forces south of the city. His command, which included most of the Virginia and Pennsylvania militia brigades, was responsible for supporting Forts Babcock, Covington, and Wood and for manning a breastwork at Ferry Point. Although an important mission, General Winder protested because his command was away from the most likely scene of action.

The Battle of Baltimore, September 12–14, 1814

On September 10, observers on Federal Hill watched as British warships scouted the mouth of the Patapsco. The next day additional vessels probed farther up the river. By noon on September 11, enemy transports and escorting warships anchored off North Point. Alarm guns sounded throughout the city.

Unlike Winder at Bladensburg, Smith intended to conduct an active defense. He directed a number of small units to reinforce the light forces already screening on the south bank of the Patapsco. He then instructed Brig. Gen. John Stricker to deploy his entire 3d Brigade forward to Patapsco Neck to delay the British as they advanced along the single road that led to the city. Numbering three thousand men, the 3d

▶ The austere grave of Brig. Gen. John Stricker in Westminster Hall and Burying Ground in Baltimore. Stricker died on June 23, 1825. (Midnightdreary/CC BY-SA 3.0)

The Chesapeake Campaign, 1813–14

Brigade consisted of five infantry regiments, a battalion of riflemen, a company of artillery, and a regiment of cavalry, all from the Baltimore area. The brigade arguably was the most capable of the three Maryland militia brigades. Stricker—Barney's brother-in-law—had served in combat during the Revolutionary War and had been called into federal service during the Whiskey Rebellion.

The brigade marched at about 1500, headed down the North Point Road. It halted at approximately 2000, just below the junction with Trappe Road, where the neck of land narrowed to less than one mile wide between Bread and Cheese Creek on the north and Bear Creek on the south. Stricker chose his ground based on previous reconnaissance. He established camp behind a strong pike-rail fence at the edge of a wood line facing a large field where, except for the cover provided by the Bouldin farm, the enemy would have to cross an open area. On the rising ground behind the clearing, Stricker set up headquarters in a Methodist meeting house. As volunteer militia companies from Hagerstown, Maryland, and Pennsylvania arrived to reinforce his brigade, he attached them to several of his subordinate regiments and prepared for battle. He ordered Capt. William B. Dyer, commanding in the place of the wounded Major Pinckney, to advance the 1st Maryland Rifle Battalion, accompanied by the 5th Maryland Cavalry. After the riflemen formed a skirmish line two miles farther down the neck, Lt. Col. James Biay led the one hundred forty troopers one mile farther, and deployed as vedettes near the Gorsuch farm.

▼ Weighing 5,700lb, this "Long Tom" gun was in combat against the British in the War of 1812, mounted on the privateer *General Armstrong*. (Naval History and Heritage Command)

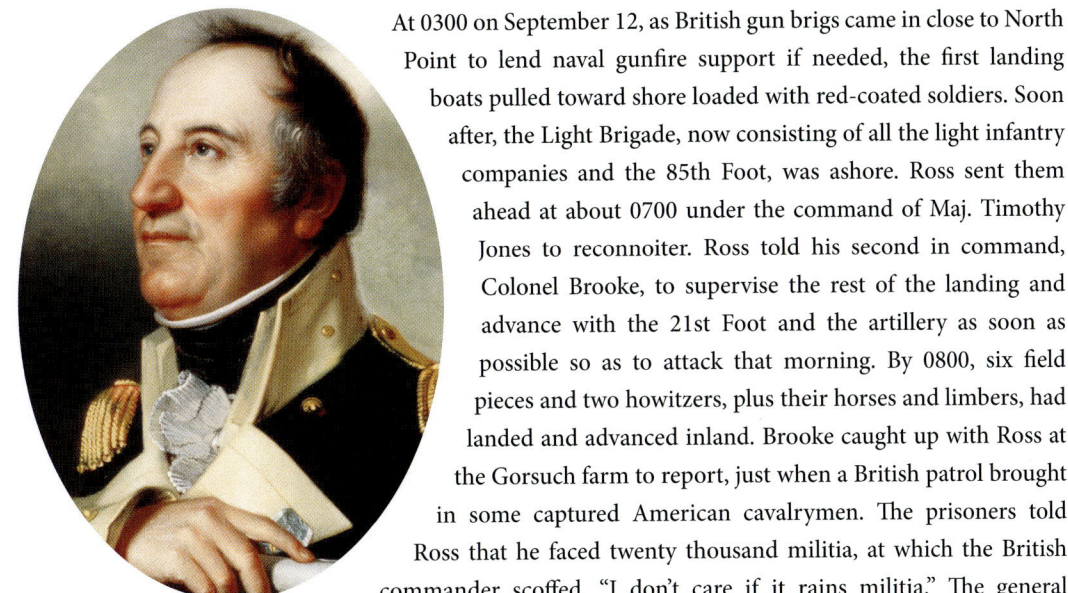

The Battle of Baltimore, September 12–14, 1814

At 0300 on September 12, as British gun brigs came in close to North Point to lend naval gunfire support if needed, the first landing boats pulled toward shore loaded with red-coated soldiers. Soon after, the Light Brigade, now consisting of all the light infantry companies and the 85th Foot, was ashore. Ross sent them ahead at about 0700 under the command of Maj. Timothy Jones to reconnoiter. Ross told his second in command, Colonel Brooke, to supervise the rest of the landing and advance with the 21st Foot and the artillery as soon as possible so as to attack that morning. By 0800, six field pieces and two howitzers, plus their horses and limbers, had landed and advanced inland. Brooke caught up with Ross at the Gorsuch farm to report, just when a British patrol brought in some captured American cavalrymen. The prisoners told Ross that he faced twenty thousand militia, at which the British commander scoffed, "I don't care if it rains militia." The general ordered Brooke to go back and hurry the troops along as American troops were probably in the area.

▲ John Stricker, by Rembrandt Peale. (Maryland Historical Society)

The cavalry vedettes had kept Stricker well informed. By 0700, he knew the British had landed. He sent his baggage back toward Baltimore and deployed his brigade in three lines, with Dyer's skirmishers to the front. He formed the first line just inside a wood astride North Point Road. Colonel Sterrett's battle-tested 5th Maryland was posted on the south side with its right flank resting on a branch of Bear Creek. Lt. Col. Kennedy Long's 27th Maryland formed on the north with its left flank extending to Bread and Cheese Creek. The six 4-pounder field guns of Capt. John Montgomery's Union Artillery Company from Baltimore straddled the road between the two infantry regiments. The position stretched a mile long. Three hundred yards to the rear, behind the west bank of Bread and Cheese Creek, Stricker deployed Lt. Col. Henry Amey's 51st Maryland on the right and Lt. Col. Benjamin Fowler's 39th Maryland on the left side of the road. One half mile farther to the rear, on Perego's Hill near Cook's Tavern, Stricker positioned Lt. Col. William McDonald's 6th Maryland in reserve (see Map 6).

Stricker planned for Dyer's riflemen to retard the enemy's progress until the two forward regiments in the first line took up the fight against the leading British units. After forcing the British to deploy into battle formation, the first line would hold as long as possible without risking becoming decisively engaged, and then withdraw through the second line to take position on the right of McDonald's regiment. The second line would then take up the battle, repeat the tactic of the first, and withdraw to McDonald's left. The reunited brigade would then engage in a fighting withdrawal back to Hampstead Hill.

▼ *The Battle of North Point*, by Don Troiani. (National Guard Heritage Painting)

75

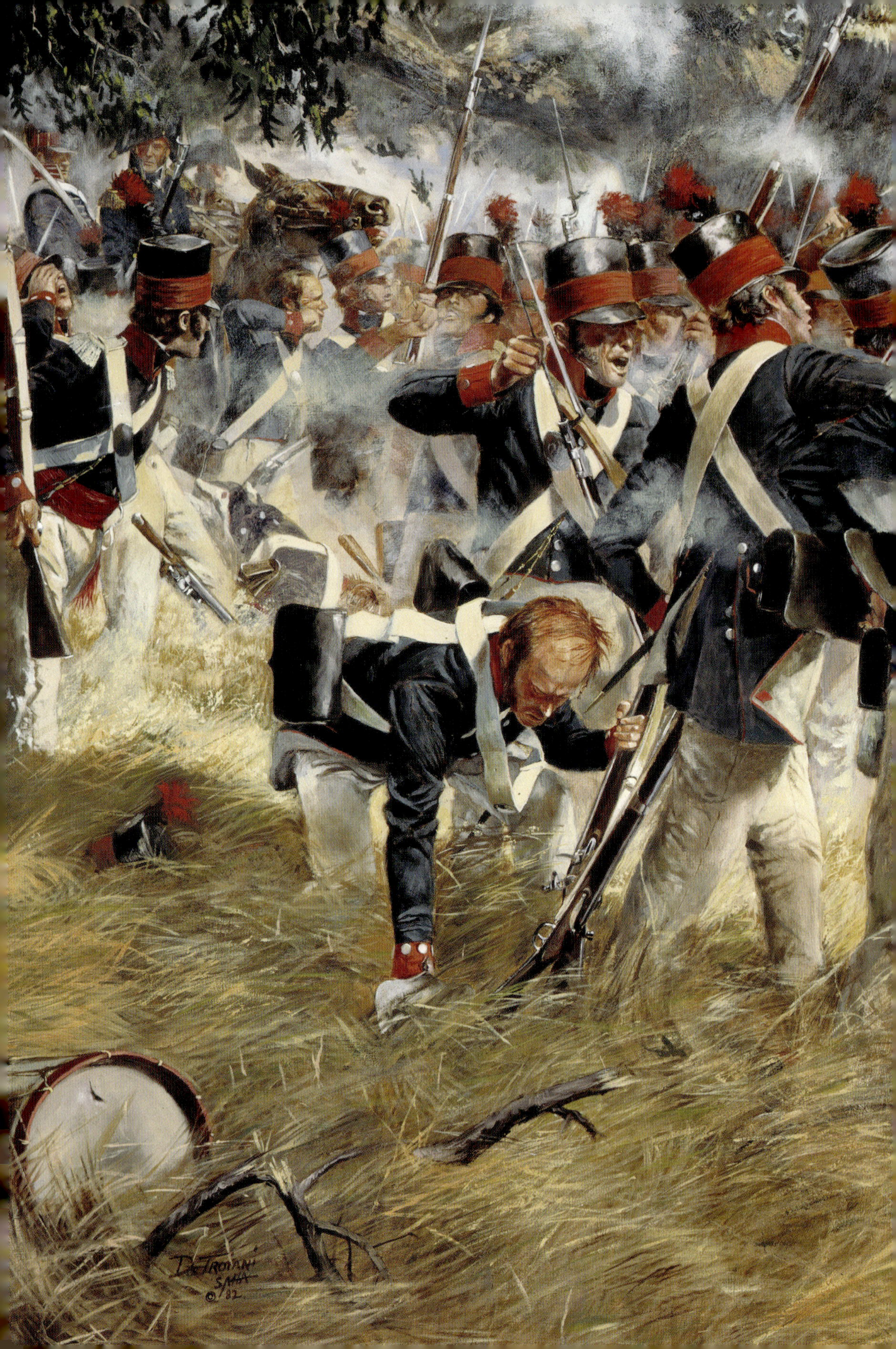
D. Troiani
SMA
© '82

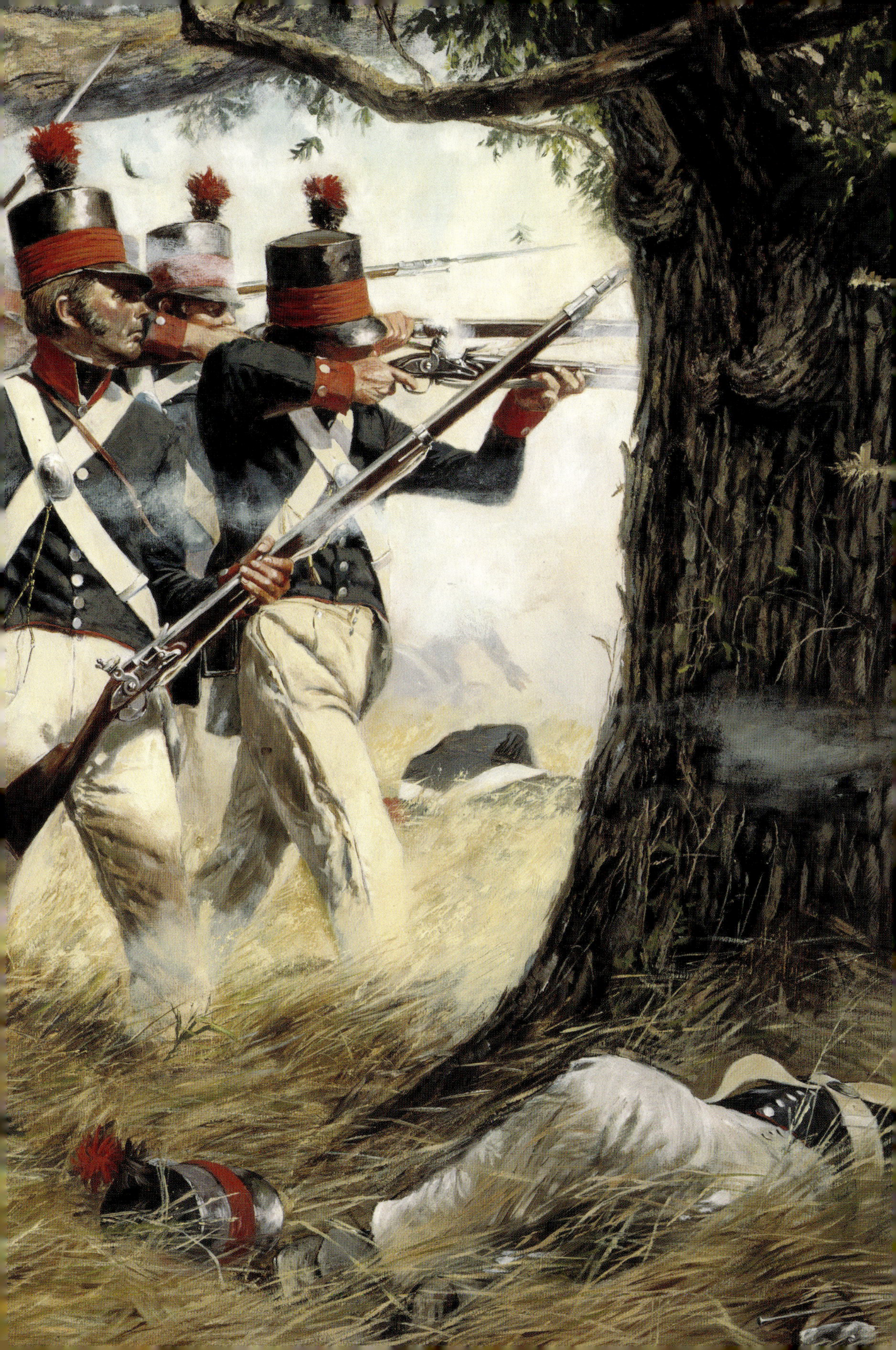

The plan got off to a rocky start. Acting on a false rumor that British marines had landed to his rear, Dyer ordered the riflemen back before they had fired a shot. Chagrinned by the unauthorized retreat, Stricker ordered Dyer and the cavalrymen who had returned from scouting to take positions on the front line to the right of the 5th Maryland. When vedettes reported that a British advance party was at the Gorsuch farmhouse, several officers of the 5th Maryland Regiment volunteered to lead their companies for a strike. Maj. Richard Heath of the 5th Maryland advanced with Capt. Aaron Levering's Independent Blues and Capt. Benjamin C. Howard's Mechanical Volunteers of that regiment, Capt. Edward Aisquith's Sharp Shooters from the rifle battalion, and Lt. John S. Styles' detachment of artillerymen with one gun. They deployed about a half mile forward, and the two hundred fifty

◀ A monument commemorating the battle of North Point at the junction of Calvert Street and Fayette Street, Baltimore, Maryland. It was designed by French-American architect Maximilian Godefroy and dedicated in 1815. (Library of Congress)

BATTLE OF BALTIMORE
September 12–14, 1814

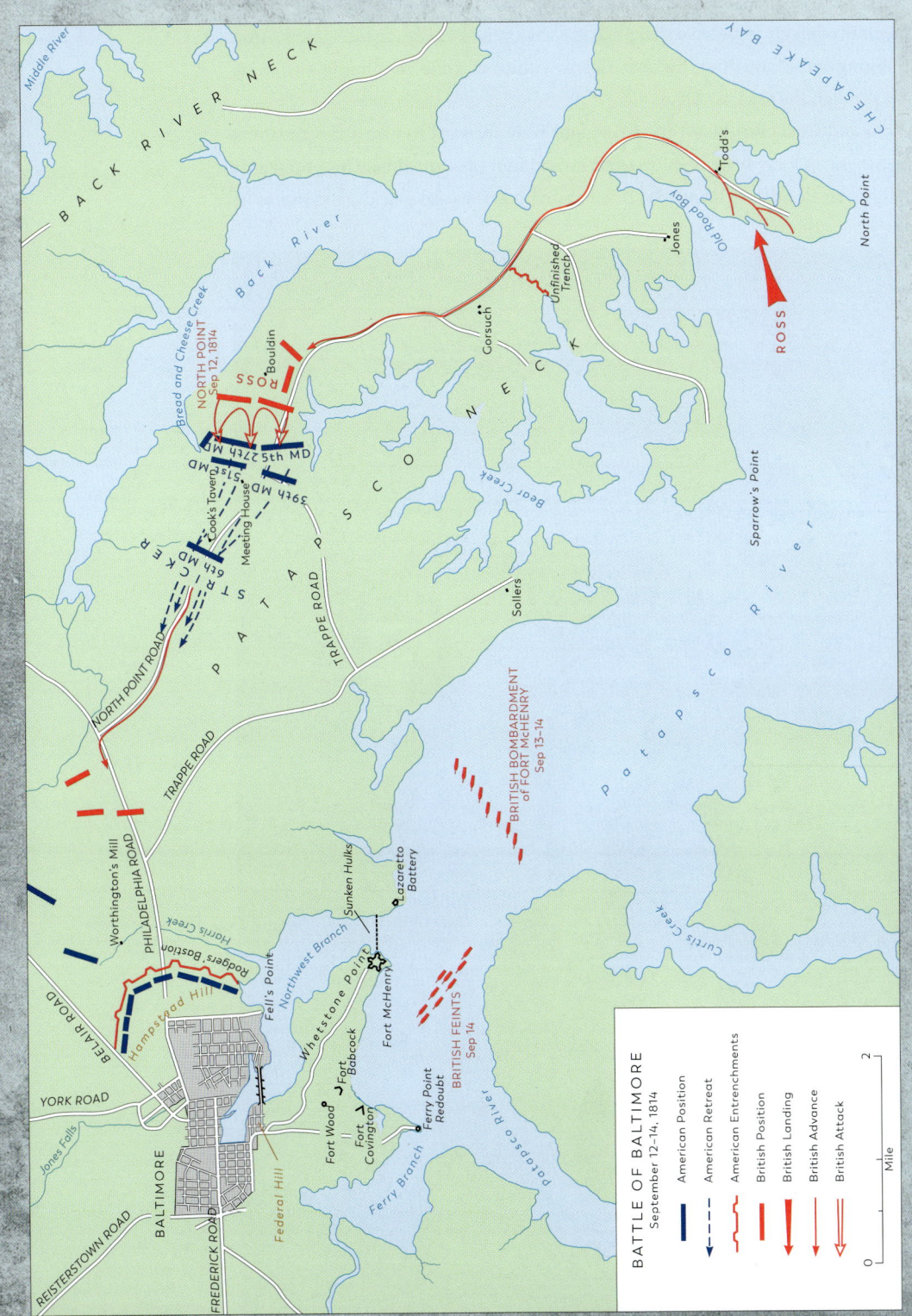

Map 6

The Chesapeake Campaign, 1813–14

Americans quickly initiated a sharp skirmish with the British advance guard. After sustaining some casualties, the Americans withdrew while continuing a running fight through the thick woods.

Ross and Cockburn heard the firing and rode forward to assess the situation. The American foray surprised Ross and caused him to overestimate his opponent's strength. He decided to bring his army's main body forward quickly, and just as he

◀ *The death of General Ross near Baltimore*, by G. M. Brighty. (Library of Congress)

turned in the saddle to tell Cockburn, a round of ball and buckshot struck him in the arm and chest. He fell from his horse mortally wounded as aides and subordinate officers rushed to his assistance. Ross died as he was carried back to the landing site for medical treatment. His death shocked the British, and Colonel Brooke assumed command. He brought up reinforcements that drove Heath's men back to the main American line. While bringing up his own artillery, Brooke perceived a "several hundred yard gap" between the American left and the Back River, and he moved to exploit it. Seeing the British move toward his left flank, Stricker ordered the 39th Maryland to the left of the 27th Maryland, and ordered the 51st Maryland to form at a right angle to protect his vulnerable left flank. Such a maneuver under fire was beyond the capabilities of the inexperienced troops, and instead of forming where Stricker wanted them, they milled about in confusion.

Sensing the moment was right to attack, at 1450 Brooke launched a furious assault concentrated on Stricker's left flank. Both sides traded volleys, but the 51st Maryland became confused and broke, taking part of the 39th Maryland along with them. While the left crumbled under the fire of Brooke's 4th Foot, the more reliable troops on Stricker's right held firm. Blasted with musketry and grapeshot, the 21st and 44th Foot suffered heavy casualties assaulting the 5th and 27th Maryland. After an hour of heavy fighting, Stricker, whose orders were to fight a delaying action, directed his infantry and artillery to fall back to join the 6th Maryland at Cook's Tavern. While the British claimed that they drove and scattered the Americans from the field, Stricker reported most of his units had re-formed. Brooke did not order his forces to exploit their success, but remained on the battlefield until the morning of September 13. Stricker listed his losses as 24 killed, 139 wounded, and 50 men captured. In addition to General Ross, the British suffered 38 killed, 251 wounded, and 50 men missing.

Having accomplished his mission, Stricker withdrew toward Worthington's Mills and took new positions as Smith had ordered. General Winder arrived with Brig. Gen. Hugh Douglass' Virginia brigade from the south of town and some regulars not deployed elsewhere, including a company of U.S. dragoons under Capt. John Burd. These forces joined Stricker on the left flank and apart from the main American line. They were positioned to attack the right flank of Brooke's army if it continued its advance on Hampstead Hill.

Following a heavy rain on the night of September 12/13, Brooke had his men moving toward Hampstead Hill at 0530. A short while later, he could hear Cochrane's bomb ships shelling Fort McHenry. When he reached the junction of the North Point and Philadelphia Roads, the sight of the American defensive line stunned Brooke. He had assumed that the force he had driven off at great cost the day before at North Point represented the main American effort. After realizing his error, he tried to maneuver toward the entrenchments on Smith's left

▼ This artwork shows the bombardment of Fort McHenry by the British on the morning of September 13, 1814. Note the high angle of the fire to increase range. Up to 1,800 shells were fired in 24 hours. (Library of Congress/PD)

A VIEW of the BOMBARDMENT of Fort McH
Observatory, under the Command of Admirals Cochrane & Cockbur
thrown from 1500 to 1800 shells, in the Night attempted to land by forci

near Baltimore, by the British fleet, taken from the
the morning of the 13th of Sepr. 1814 which lasted 24 hours, &
sage up the ferry branch but were repulsed with great loss.

J. Bower, sc. Philr.

References.
A, Fort McHenry.
B, Lazaretto.
C, Salauave House
D, Admiral Ship. North Point
E, Ferry and Fort.

The Chesapeake Campaign, 1813–14

flank, and immediately encountered Winder's and Stricker's men arrayed on high ground in prepared positions above the Belair Road. When Brooke withdrew back toward the Philadelphia Road, Stricker and Winder advanced their brigades in a demonstration that threatened his rear. By the afternoon of September 13, Brooke was content with merely sending patrols to probe Smith's main line for weaknesses, possibly for a risky night attack.

The Battle of Baltimore, September 12–14, 1814

Admiral Cochrane believed that if he could pound Baltimore's harbor defenses into submission, his ships could enter the harbor and enfilade the Hampstead Hill line with their naval guns to assist Brooke in driving off the American defenders. Due to the shallowness of the river, Cochrane only advanced one frigate, five bomb ships, and one rocket-firing ship toward Fort McHenry. Each bomb vessel had one 10-inch and one 13-inch mortar that could fire a 200-pound exploding shell or an incendiary carcass every five minutes. They began firing toward Fort McHenry from nearly two and a half miles away by 0700. When the defenders attempted to reply with their larger-caliber guns, they realized the mortars' greater range allowed the British to remain beyond their reach and ceased firing by 1000. The British continued their bombardment against the fort, but Cochrane could tell that his weapons were not having the desired effect. He wrote to Cockburn who was ashore with Brooke: "It is impossible for the Ships to render you any assistance ... It is for Colonel Brooke to consider ... whether he has Force sufficient to defeat so large a number as it [is] said the Enemy has collected; say 20,000 strong or even less number & to take the Town."

Meanwhile, large bombs continued to fall inside the fort's walls or to explode overhead. Captain Evans saw two men killed by shell fragments as they hid under a heavy gun. He also stated that he saw a woman carrying water vaporized as a shell hit her. He noted that some shells "as big as a flour barrel" fell nearby and failed to explode. At 1400, a shell scored a direct hit on bastion number four and its 24-pounder, killing Lt. Levi Clagett and Sgt. John Clemm of the Baltimore Fencibles and wounding a number of others. When Cochrane ordered his bomb ships closer, the move brought them within range of the fort's larger guns. After American fire damaged two bomb ships and damaged the rocket ship so

◀ This photograph from the 1860s show two soldiers aside a 13in mortar, almost as wide as it is tall. The fused explosive shells they fired weighed around 200lb. (Library of Congress/PD)

The Chesapeake Campaign, 1813–14

badly that it had to be towed to safety by the accompanying frigate, the admiral ordered his vessels to retire to a safer distance.

Cochrane continued long-range firing through the night and into the early morning hours of September 14. After considering his options, Cochrane ordered Capt. Charles Napier of H.M.S. *Euryalis* to lead twenty ship's boats loaded with nearly twelve hundred sailors and marines in an attempt to slip into Ferry Branch

◀ A portrait of Vice Admiral Sir George Cockburn, one of the great British naval commanders of the Napoleonic era. In this artwork, he wears the sword which was presented to him by Horatio Nelson in 1797. (National Maritime Museum, Greenwich/PD)

The Battle of Baltimore, September 12–14, 1814

▲ The 24-pounder cannon was a standard heavy artillery piece used between the 17th and the 19th centuries. It was typically a naval gun, mounted on ships of the line, but it could also be found in coastal defenses. (James Yolkowski/CC BY-SA 2.0 CA)

▼ The 1814 cartoon "John Bull and the Baltimoreans," by artist William Charles, shows the humiliation of British forces by the doughty people of Baltimore. The figure of John Bull declares: "Mercy! mercy on me—What fellows those Baltimoreans are—After the example of the Alexandrians I thought I had nothing to do but enter the Town and carry off the Booty—And here is nothing but Defeat and Disgrace!!!" (Library of Congress/PD)

and threaten Fort McHenry from its landward side. Under a driving rain, eleven of the boats became separated and drifted toward the Lazaretto, where Lieutenant Frazier's flotillamen and nearby Pennsylvania riflemen prepared to repel the landing. On realizing their mistake, the British pulled back toward their fleet. The nine remaining boats continued up Ferry Branch until detected by the men at Fort Babcock. They opened fire and were soon followed by the guns at Fort Covington. Sailing Master Webster later stated, "I could hear the balls from our guns strike the barges. My men stated to me that they could hear the shrieks of the wounded. ... During the firing of the enemy, I could distinctly see their barges by the explosion of their cannon which was a great guide to me to fire by." The other batteries in and around Fort McHenry added their fire to punish Napier's force as it retreated.

By 0400, September 14, the British firing began to slacken. At 0700 it ceased altogether. Soldiers on Hampstead Hill worried the fort had fallen, but the post had withstood the onslaught. Georgetown lawyer and militia lieutenant Francis Scott Key had been taken aboard a British flagship to assist in negotiating Dr. Beanes' release. Key, Beanes, and Col. John Skinner, the American prisoner-exchange agent, witnessed the nightlong bombardment with fearful anticipation. After the firing had ceased in the morning, Key saw the large garrison flag flying from the fort's flagstaff. The three Americans knew that the men in the fort had prevailed.

The Chesapeake Campaign, 1813–14

The Battle of Baltimore, September 12–14, 1814

The Chesapeake Campaign, 1813–14

The sight inspired Key to write the poem he originally titled "The Defense of Fort McHenry," which he later renamed "The Star-Spangled Banner." It became the national anthem of the United States in 1931. Skinner and Key's mission ultimately succeeded in obtaining Beanes' release.

With naval forces unable to outflank Hampstead Hill, Brooke's only options were to conduct an unsupported attack against a strongly entrenched enemy or to retreat. After weighing the advantages and disadvantages, he decided on withdrawal. As his army marched back toward North Point, Brooke halted in an attempt to lure the Americans into a battle in the open. Smith, however, resisted the temptation to leave the trenches. By September 15, Cochrane's ships reembarked the exhausted troops. British operations in the Chesapeake had effectively ended for the season. Before long, Cochrane headed to Halifax, and Cockburn departed for Bermuda. The British retained their naval base and a small contingent of colonial marines on Tangier Island until March 1815, the month following ratification of the Treaty of Ghent, which ended the war.

◄ *By Dawn's Early Light* depicts Francis Scott Key with outstretched arm toward the flag at Fort McHenry, by Edward Percy Moran. (Maryland Historical Society)

Analysis

The British had launched their Chesapeake campaign to serve as a diversion, not an invasion. Their operations, however, failed to compel the United States to redeploy its Regular Army from the Canadian theater.

Analysis

Allegedly stating that the nervous citizens of the Chesapeake should not expect the Regular Army to "defend every man's turnip patch," Secretary of War John Armstrong had chosen to leave the defense of the region largely to the militia. The raid on Washington, while a propaganda coup, likewise failed to disrupt the U.S. government. In his official report, Admiral Cochrane stated that he never actually wanted to take the economically more important city of Baltimore. The operation to capture America's third-largest city and thriving commercial center resulted in a failure that cost the lives of more than fifty British soldiers, including General Ross, and numerous wounded. The resolute defense surprised British commanders who had come to expect easy victories, and proved that American regulars and militiamen, when ably led and adequately trained, were equal to the soldiers of the British Empire. News of America's nearly simultaneous victories at Baltimore and Plattsburgh, New York, where a combined U.S. land and naval force had repelled an invasion down Lake Champlain, contributed to Britain's decision to end the war without seeking any territorial concessions from the United States.

▼ This finely detailed artwork shows the damage to the U.S. Capitol building after the British had attempted to burn it down in August 1814. Sections of the building are shored up with wood to prevent them falling down. (Library of Congress)

Further Reading

Benn, Carl. *The War of 1812*. Oxford: Osprey Publishing, 2024

Black, Jeremy. *The War of 1812 in the Age of Napoleon*. London: Continuum, 2010.

Daughan, George C. *1812: The Navy's War*. New York: Basic Books, 2011.

Eshelman, Ralph E., Scott S. Sheads, and Donald R. Hickey. *The War of 1812 in the Chesapeake: A Reference Guide to Historic Sites in Maryland, Virginia, and the District of Columbia*. Baltimore, Ma.: Johns Hopkins University Press, 2010.

Eshelman, Ralph E., and Burton K. Kummerow. *In Full Glory Reflected: Discovering the War of 1812 in the Chesapeake*. Baltimore: Maryland Historical Society Press, 2012.

Esposito, Gabriele. *Armies of the War of 1812: The Armies of the United States, United Kingdom and Canada from 1812 to 1815*. Point Pleasant, NJ: Winged Hussar Publishing, 2019.

George, Christopher T. *Terror on the Chesapeake: The War of 1812 on the Bay*. Shippensburg, Pa.: White Mane Press, 2001.

Gregg, Adams. *U.S. Soldier vs British Soldier: War of 1812*. Oxford: Osprey Publishing, 2021.

Lord, Walter. *The Dawn's Early Light*. New York: W. W. Norton, 1972.

Pitch, Anthony S. *The Burning of Washington: The British Invasion of 1814*. Annapolis, Md.: Naval Institute Press, 1998.

Sheads, Scott S. *The Chesapeake Campaigns 1813–15: Middle Ground of the War of 1812*. Oxford: Osprey Publishing, 2013.

Smith, Gene Allen. *The Slaves' Gamble: Choosing Sides in the War of 1812*. New York: Palgrave Macmillan, 2013.

Vogel, Steve. *Through the Perilous Fight: Six Weeks That Saved the Nation*. New York: Random House, 2013.

Whitehorne, Joseph A. *The Battle for Baltimore: 1814*. Baltimore: Nautical and Aviation Publishing Company of America, 1997.

Index

Addison, Capt. William H. 64, 67
Alexandria 7, 14, 30, 45, 57
ammunition 60
Annapolis, Maryland 33, 41, 42, 47
Armstrong, Secretary of War John 30, 33, 38, 39, 41, 46, 47, 54, 59, 93

Baltimore Fencibles 63
Baltimore, battle of 7, 73–91
Baltimore, Maryland 7, 10, 12, 30, 33, 37, 41, 46, 59, 62–67, 69, 73–91, 93
Barney, Master Commandant Joshua 7, 37–40, 43–46, 49, 50–51, 54
Bathurst, Lord Henry Bathurst 6, 10
Beall, Col. William 51, 54
Beanes, Dr. William 61, 87, 91
Bear Creek 74, 75
Beatty, Lt. Col. Henry 21, 23, 25
Beckwith, Col. Sir Thomas S. 19, 23–26, 28, 35
Benedict 7, 39, 41, 43, 45, 46, 50, 56
Bladensburg, Maryland 7, 46, 47, 48, 49, 50–54, 59, 69, 71
bomb ships 38, 44, 57, 81, 85
Bomford, Capt. George 30
Bowlingly Plantation 35, 36
Bread and Cheese Creek 74, 75, 79
British forces
 1st, or Light Brigade 48, 51–52, 54, 75
 2d Brigade 48, 51, 52
 3d Brigade 48, 51, 55
 102d Regiment of Foot 19, 33
 21st Regiment of Foot 42, 48, 75, 81
 44th Regiment of Foot 42, 48, 52, 53, 81
 4th Regiment of Foot 42, 48, 52, 53, 81
 85th Regiment of Foot 42, 48, 51–52, 75

Brooke, Col. Arthur 48, 52–53, 75, 81–85, 91

Calvert County 33, 38, 42
Carberry, Col. Henry 37, 38, 39, 40, 47
Cassin, Capt. John 20, 25
cavalry 33, 50, 74, 75, 78
Celey Road 25, 26
Centipede 24
Chesapeake Bay 6, 7, 10, 12, 17, 18, 29, 33
Cochrane, V. Adm. Sir Alexander 28, 29, 37, 41, 42, 44, 46, 48, 50, 62, 85–86, 91, 93
Cockburn, R. Adm. George 6, 7, 10, 12–15, 17–18, 25, 28, 30, 33, 36, 37–38, 41–46, 50, 55, 62, 80, 81, 85, 86, 91
Concord Point 13, 15
Congreve, Sir William 13, 16
Cook's Tavern 75, 79, 81
Craney Island, battle of 7, 19–27

Elizabeth River 12, 19, 21
Evans, Capt. Frederick 63, 85

fleche 66
flotillamen 40, 46, 63, 64, 66, 71, 87
Fort Babcock 64, 66, 72, 87
Fort Covington 66, 72, 79, 87
Fort McHenry 14, 63–64, 66, 71, 79, 81, 82–83, 85, 87, 90–91
Fort Mifflin 63
Fort Nelson 12, 19, 27
Fort Norfolk 12, 19, 27
Fort Warburton 30, 58–59
Fort Washington 7, 30, 44, 45, 46, 57, 58–59
Fort Wood 66

fortifications 10–11, 12, 21, 41, 47, 64, 67, 68, 69, 71, 72
Fredericktown 17, 18

Georgetown 7, 14, 17, 18, 30, 45, 54
Gleig, Lt. George 51
Godefroy, J. Maximilian M. 68, 78
Gordon, Capt. James A. 44, 57

Halifax, Nova Scotia 26, 36, 91
Hampstead Hill 67, 71, 72, 75, 81, 85, 91
Hampton 19, 25–27
Hampton, battle of 25–27
Havre de Grace 13, 14, 15, 18

Independent Companies of Foreigners 19, 26
infantry 30–31, 48, 51, 60

Jarvis, Sgt. James 23, 25
Jones, Secretary of the Navy William 20, 38, 39, 44, 46

Kent Island 14, 33, 59
Kettle Bottom Shoals 14, 30, 44, 45
Kinsale 14, 42

Lazaretto Point 63, 71, 79, 87
Long Old Fields, battle of 44–48
Lottery 6, 10
Lower Marlboro 7, 39, 45

Madison, Present James 40–41, 50, 57
Miller, Capt. Samuel 38, 40, 44, 46, 51, 54
Monroe, Secretary of State James 32, 33, 48, 51, 54, 59, 69

Nicholson, Maj. William H. 33–35
Norfolk, Virginia 10, 18, 19–20, 25, 27, 30, 37

The Chesapeake Campaign, 1813–14

North Point Road 74, 75
North Point, battle of 7, 73–81
Northeast River 15, 18
Nottingham, Maryland 14, 39, 42, 43, 45

O'Neill, Lt. John 15

Parker, Capt. Sir Peter 59–60
Patapsco River 12, 14, 33, 63, 67, 73
Patuxent River 14, 37, 40, 41, 43, 44, 45
Pechell, Capt. Samuel G. 24, 25
Pig Point 14, 43, 44, 45
Porter, Capt. David 46, 57
Portsmouth Island 21, 28
Portsmouth, Virginia 10, 12, 14, 20, 21
Potato Battery 13, 15
Potomac River 28, 30, 41, 42, 44, 45, 46, 48, 49, 53, 57
Prevost, Lt. Gen. Sir George 41

Queenstown 7, 33, 35

raids 12, 13, 15, 17, 28, 33, 37, 39, 41, 42, 48, 57, 59, 93
Rappahannock River 14, 18, 41
Reed, Lt. Col. Philip 59–60
Ross, Maj. Gen. Robert 7, 42–49, 50–52, 54–55, 57, 61, 62, 75

Sea Fencibles 64, 65, 71
Smith, Brig. Gen. Walter 46, 47, 51
Smith, Maj. Gen. Samuel 13, 46, 62–64, 67–72
St. Leonard Creek 37, 40
St. Leonard, Maryland 7, 37, 40, 45
St. Mary's City, Maryland 14, 30, 33
St. Michaels, Maryland 14, 33, 36

Stansbury, Brig. Gen. Tobias 46, 48, 50–53, 72
Stewart, Capt. Charles 20
Stricker, Brig. Gen. John 73–75, 78, 81, 84
Susquehanna River 13, 14, 15

Tangier Island 14, 27, 36, 37, 91
Taylor, Brig. Gen. Robert B. 20, 21, 23
the Thoroughfare (strait) 21, 23
Thornton, Col. William 48, 51–53
Turncliff Bridge 51, 53, 54

U.S. forces
  1st Brigade of the Columbian Division 46, 47, 50
  1st Marine Artillery of the Union 71–72
  1st Maryland Brigade 72
  1st Maryland Regiment 46–47, 71
  11th Maryland Brigade 72
  2d Brigade of the Columbian Division 46
  2d Maryland Regiment 46–47
  3d Maryland Brigade 73–74
  3d Virginia Regiment 23
  5th Regiment, Maryland Volunteer Infantry 47, 52–53, 75, 78, 79, 81
  5th Virginia Regiment 23
  12th Militia Brigade 33
  14th U.S. Infantry 69
  14th Virginia Brigade 42
  20th U.S. Infantry 23
  21st Maryland Regiment 59
  31st Maryland Regiment 38
  36th U.S. Infantry 30, 37–42, 46, 53, 69
  38th Maryland Regiment 33

  38th U.S. Infantry 30, 38, 40–42, 46, 53, 69
  45th Maryland Regiment 38
  47th Virginia Regiment 42
  49th Maryland Regiment 17
  4th Virginia Regiment 23
  60th Virginia Regiment 47
  Portsmouth Light Artillery 23
U.S.S. *Constellation* 7, 12, 20, 21, 25, 37
U.S.S. *Constitution* 20
Upper Marlboro 14, 44, 45, 47, 56, 61

vedette 50, 74, 75, 78
Virginia's Coan River 7, 42

Wadsworth, Col. Decius 30, 38–40, 50
Warren, Adm. Sir John Borlase 10, 12, 18, 19, 24–25, 28, 30, 36, 37
warships 10, 13, 20, 37, 38, 40, 48, 56, 57, 65, 73
Washington, D.C. 10, 16, 22, 28, 38, 39, 41, 42–49, 50, 53, 54, 56, 57, 93
weapons
  10-inch mortar 85
  13-inch mortar 85
  18-pounder gun 23, 38, 40, 63, 66
  24-pounder gun 20, 23, 56, 85, 87
  32-pounder gun 15, 20
  4-pounder field guns 75
  42-pounder gun 64
  Congreve rockets 13, 16, 23, 24, 52
  muskets 69
Whiskey Rebellion, the 63, 74
Winder, Brig. Gen. William H. 41, 42, 44, 46, 48–9, 50–51, 52, 54, 69
Winder, Governor Levin 62, 69

Yeocomico River 14, 42